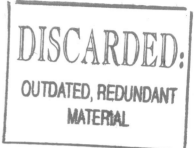

Date: 7/12/11

D1509014

SHAPE UP!
100 CONDITIONING SWIM WORKOUTS

Blythe Lucero

Meyer & Meyer Sport

British Library Cataloguing in Publication Data
A catalogue record for this book is available from the British Library

Shape Up! 100 Conditioning Swim Workouts
Maidenhead: Meyer & Meyer Sport (UK) Ltd., 2010
ISBN 978-1-84126-269-7

© 2010 by Meyer & Meyer Sport (UK) Ltd.
Aachen, Adelaide, Auckland, Budapest, Cape Town, Graz, Indianapolis,
Maidenhead, Olten (CH), Singapore, Toronto
Member of the World
Sport Publishers' Association (WSPA)
www.w-s-p-a.org
Printed by: B.O.S.S Druck und Medien GmbH
ISBN: 978-1-84126-269-7
E-Mail: info@m-m-sports.com
www.m-m-sports.com

TABLE OF CONTENTS

INTRODUCTION

I have always looked at writing a workout like cooking a good dinner. As I plan the menu, I think about whom I am preparing it for. I am aware that what I serve will be experienced as it is consumed. I know that ultimately what I cook will help healthy growth and development. So, when I cook a meal, or write a workout, my goal is to make it appetizing, filling and full of nutrition. Like a meal, if a workout isn't interesting, chances are it will not be met with enthusiasm, or even finished. The same old menu day after day gets boring. Spicing things up with interesting presentations, combinations and tasty treats makes it more exciting and palatable. Further, just as with dinner, a workout must be served in the right portion sizes. Too little, and it is unsatisfying, and won't supply the body with what it needs. Too much, and it is overwhelming, leading to either excessive consumption or waste. Finally, just as a well-balanced meal contains a variety of food groups, rich in vitamins and minerals, a good workout must contain a blend of elements that together fuel the body, mind and spirit.

When I cook and when I prepare workouts, I use skill, creativity and love! In the kitchen, I deliberately blend certain ingredients, which I have learned from other recipes taste good together. Likewise, when I write workouts, I assemble specific elements together that I know from experience produce positive results. When I am cooking, I use color, texture, aroma and taste to create the richest sensory experience possible. Similarly, when I plan a workout, I strive to design a composition that is engaging, stimulating and meaningful to the athlete. Finally, when I cook, and when I write workouts, it is a labor of love. I am passionate about the process, and I am passionate about the results. It is my constant hope that this comes through in every meal, and every workout I prepare.

This is the second in a three book series called "Coach Blythe's Swim Workouts." This book contains conditioning-based workouts designed to help swimmers shape up by building swimming capacity and accessible power. The first book in the series contains technique-based workouts, designed to help swimmers improve swimming efficiency by improving swimming mechanics. The third book in the series contains challenging workouts, designed for advanced level training. Swimmers may use the material in these books to build their fitness, or to train for competitive swimming or triathlon on their own, when their coach is not present. These books can also be useful to coaches looking for workout content to use in the training programs they design for their swimmers.

Without the intent of discouraging anyone taking up the wonderful sport of swimming, this book is neither a 'Learn to Swim' manual, nor a 'Swimming Technique' guide. Users of this book are expected to have the ability to move safely through the water, and have an under-standing, both in theory and practice of swimming mechanics. Always consult a doctor before beginning a fitness routine such as this.

The 100 workouts in this book focus on shaping up with swimming, using a strategy that builds endurance, strength and versatility over time. This collection of workouts is presented in a sequence that when done regularly, will encourage gradual adaptation, and progress towards one's fitness goals. The workouts range from 2,200 to 3,500 yards/meters. Specific workouts are included for each of the com-petitive swimming strokes. Each workout is designed as a balanced practice session unto itself, but also as a part of a long-term program of physical conditioning.

So, if you are ready, dig in! Bon Appetit.

GETTING THE MOST OUT OF THIS BOOK

Swimming to Shape Up

What does the term "Shape Up" mean to you? Beyond improved fitness, this term might bring to mind more specific goals such as weight loss, lower body fat, toning, more strength, improved cardiovascular health or stress reduction. Swimming can be an excellent method to achieve any of these goals. It can be also be totally ineffective.

Experts commonly agree that swimming is one of the best fitness activities a person can engage in to achieve full body fitness. However, it takes ongoing activity to make a difference. One or two swims will just not do it. Further, how and what one swims is also an important factor in the quality of result. Health professionals disagree about the effectiveness of swimming as a way shed weight, for example. Why? Because, it is possible for two swimmers, both swimming for one hour, to burn vastly different numbers of calories, simply due to what and how they swim. Finally, the mechanics of swimming plays a very important role in an individual's ability to benefit from a swimming fitness routine. Good swimming technique will allow a swimmer to expend less energy, and therefore be able to continue to swim for a longer period of time. On the other hand, poor technique will make a swimmer too exhausted to maintain the activity long enough to achieve fitness benefits.

This collection of workouts uses established training methods of swimming to build fitness. As you gain physical conditioning, and begin to shape up, I hope you find swimming to be as rewarding as I have, and stick with it. Over time, as you use this book to work toward your particular goals, you might just find that you achieve additional results serendipitously along the way.

Make the Commitment

Like any effective fitness routine, swimming requires personal dedication to get results. Think of personal dedication as a mindset, which includes characteristics such as patience, perseverance and commitment. In order to get the most out of this book to Shape Up effectively with swimming, you must be ready to put in the time and effort, and be prepared to keep working at it, even though it will take time. You must maintain your motivation to achieve results, slowly but surely. You must believe in what you are doing.

To shape up with swimming, you must make a three-part commitment:

Commitment to swim regularly over time

To shape up with swimming, you will need to swim frequently. Plan a routine that makes time for three to four swims per week, expecting to be in the water for an hour at minimum each time. It will take some time to adjust to this routine. At first you might feel pretty tired. But after you establish a base, your routine will become much more enjoyable, and rewarding. As everyone is different, there is no exact answer to how long it will take to get to this point, but plan on several weeks of base work. When you do begin to see results, this is not a cue to ease up, but a sign that what you are doing is starting to work. Keep it up!

Commitment to follow the workouts

The workouts in this book are designed to build well-rounded fitness, with a comprehensive and balanced program of progressive, diversi-fied swims. You have to be willing to follow the workouts... even when no one is looking! It is easy to skip and edit workouts. It is exactly like leaving the vegetables uneaten on your dinner plate. You will not get all the elements you need to develop fully if you leave something out. Certain activities will be more challenging than others. These are the very activities that you should focus your energy on. By building your weak areas, in addition to your strong areas, you will develop more balanced conditioning and well-rounded fitness.

Commitment to maintain good technique

Good swimming technique is the foundation of good swimming. Without constant attention to this issue, even the efforts of an experienced, refined swimmer can be derailed. When swimming workouts, especially without a coach present, it is easy to fall into bad habits. If not noticed and corrected early, stroke errors can become reinforced as they are repeated, stroke after stroke, leading to slower progress and potential injury. While stroke problems can be frustrating, and it is tempting to simply ignore them, and muscle your way through your workout, take time to analyze and identify them. Maintaining stroke quality is a must!

Once you have decided to make the commitment, and hold on to the mindset of personal dedication to your goals, you are ready to embark on an effective "Shape Up" swimming program.

Shape Up Strategy

The workouts in this book are neither random, nor generic. Each is part of a strategy designed to result in better physical fitness, conditioning and swimming capacity when done frequently and progressively, and over time. The Shape Up Strategy employed in this book is based on three key principles that are the core of this coaches' training philosophy:

1. **Full body fitness requires full body training**

   Successful development of full body fitness comes from building strength, as well as endurance. Training one without the other only produces limited success. Because swimming, by nature, requires both strength and endurance, it is an excellent method to train full body fitness. When we do the repetitive action, resistance-based activity of swimming, our muscles require an increased supply of oxygen to exert and to keep working. The lungs have to build capacity to meet the demand of exchanging more new and used air. As more new oxygen is be drawn into the lungs, and carried through the bloodstream to the heart, the heart muscle also has to increase its pumping capacity, to supply new oxygen-rich blood to the muscles at work, and, to carry depleted blood away from the muscles. As this chain of systems adapts to the demands of exercise, fitness level rises. Working interdependently, these systems build capacity for increased workload and therefore potential results.

2. Fitness develops in stages

To swim for any length of time, you must possess both strength and endurance. Yet, to develop the strength to perform the activity, you must have the endurance to practice it, and, to develop the endurance to practice the activity, you must have the strength to perform it. So, if the development of each is dependent on the other, how can it ever be achieved or improved upon? The answer is: in stages. We must build our capacity for strength and endurance gradually. It is a process of building one's tolerance for work, through progressions of specific and structured stress and recovery. The process involves pushing the body's tolerance for work beyond what it is used to, then allowing the body to rest. As it recovers, the body adapts to that level of work. Then, the workload can be increased, with the goal of further adaptation. How quickly one adapts is a very individual matter. A number of factors contribute the rate of adaptation, including the state of one's fitness at the start of a program, age, and coordination, among others. While these factors are, for the most part, beyond our control, we can actively affect how often we exercise, and the quality of our fitness program. Frequency is one of the most important factors in developing fitness, and, the quality and structure of the exercise is important in successfully adapting to a progressive exercise routine.

3. Versatility encourages well-rounded fitness

The ability to apply endurance and strength to different situations is often overlooked as a measure of fitness. In reality, one's ability to use strength and endurance "in action," in situations beyond training, is the ultimate measure of fitness. This is versatility, and in swimming it is developed by including a variety distances, speeds and strokes in the training content. As an example, we all have a pre-disposition to either be sprinters or distance swimmers, by the amount of fast or slow twitch muscle fibers we naturally possess. However, in fact, one's natural ability to sprint or endure only accounts for about 20% of the body's muscle fibers. The rest–that is, most of our muscle fiber- is "convertible" or trainable for speed or endurance. So, a natural sprinter can gain endurance through training, and a person with natural endurance can gain speed through training. Further, as the unique path of each different stroke works slightly different parts of the muscles, by diversifying strokes we can achieve more well-rounded muscle development. The result of training variety is a more complete and balanced development of applicable strength and endurance.

So, the Shape Up Strategy at the heart of this collection of workouts is about building. Building increased swimming capacity, building applicable power, and, building well-rounded fitness. It is a strategy that calls for a multi-dimensional approach to training with swimming. With the goal of targeting both the cardiovascular and muscular systems to progressively adapt to a variety of demands, each workout is constructed with activities and combinations of activities that build endurance, strength and versatility.

BUILDING ENDURANCE

Endurance refers to the body's ability to keep going. Examples include the ability to swim continuously, the ability to hold a pace, and the ability to accomplish more yardage. Several training techniques will be used in this workout collection to build endurance. These include:

- **Interval Training**
  Multiple short swims with a minor rest between each
- **Speed Play**
  Alternating fast and easy periods of effort during a continuous swim
- **Timed Distance Swims**
  Swimming as far as possible in a set time
- **Increasing Yardage**
  Progressively building the distance accomplished at a workout

BUILDING STRENGTH

Strength refers to the body's ability to apply power. Examples include the ability to sprint, the ability to use fewer strokes to cross the pool, and the ability to swim with intensity. Several training techniques will be used in his workout collection to build strength. These include:

- **Benchmark Swims**
  100% effort timed swims
- **Sprint Sets**
  Velocity repeats at high speed with long rest
- **Leg Burners**
  All out speed kicking sets
- **Efficiency Drills**
  Exercises that reinforce using the largest muscles possible to move farther per stroke

BUILDING VERSATILITY

Versatility refers to the body's ability to successfully perform under a variety of circumstances. Examples include the ability to effectively swim different distances at different speeds, and with different strokes. Several training techniques will be used in this workout collection to build versatility. These include:

- **Training all distances**
  Practicing distances from 25 yards to one mile
- **Training all speeds**
  Swimming at various exertion levels
- **Training all strokes**
  Including butterfly, backstroke, breaststroke and freestyle in the content of the workouts

Achieving Results

There are two ways to look at achieving results. The first way is to focus on the end result, when you have reached the goal you made when you began your fitness routine. The second way is to look at your progress along the road toward that goal. Both are important.

What a wonderful day it will be when you accomplish your goal! But even for the most determined person, keeping a long-term goal constantly in focus is sometimes difficult. Because shaping up is a process, and doesn't happen all at once, at times the ultimate goal can seem far away, even unattainable. By also looking at each step of progress along the way to the goal as an achievement itself, the goal remains more real. Seeing clear evidence that you are making progress also makes it a wonderful day.

Keeping Track of Your Swimming Progress

In order to keep track of your progress, you must measure your swimming along the way. This collection of workouts includes a number of opportunities to compare your efforts to previous efforts of the same swimming content. At the end of Chapter 2, you will find a section called "Swimmer's Progress Log," in which you can record your swimming times and other indications of progress. You will have the opportunity to establish your swimming times early on, then, about every fifth workout, opportunities for comparison will be provided. These include:

Benchmark Swims

Opportunities to time yourself for distances of 50, 100 and 200 are included for all strokes, in addition to 500 and a mile in freestyle.

Timed Distance Swims

You will be asked to swim for 5, 10 and 15 minutes, using freestyle, with the goal of swimming as far as possible within the time.

Interval Sets

You will compare both your average swim time and your rest interval for a set of 10 x 50, and 5 x 100 of freestyle, backstroke and breast-stroke, as well as 8 x 25 and 8 x 50 of butterfly.

Workouts

You will track your total workout yardage, and the length of time each workout took.

INDICATIONS OF PROGRESS

You can also track your progress in terms of physical changes, including:

Heart Rate

Tracking your heart rate is an excellent indicator of conditioning progress. You can measure:

RESTING HEART RATE

Before you get out of bed in the morning, take your pulse for 15 seconds. Multiply that number by 4 to give you your resting heart rate. As conditioning increases, your resting heart rate should go down a bit.

TARGET HEART RATE RANGE

Your optimal range of heart rate during training should be about 65% of your maximum heart rate. You can easily calculate your target heart rate (THR) with the following formula:

$$(220 - \text{Your Age}) \times 0.65 = \text{THR}$$

You can check your THR after a set by placing two fingers either on the arteries on the palm side of your wrist, or at the side of your neck, just under the jaw. Count your pulse for 6 seconds then multiply by 10. This will give you your heart rate for one minute. This formula allows you to measure your heart rate quickly. This is important because your heart rate will go down soon after you stop swimming. As you gain conditioning, you will find that you will be able to swim faster and farther while staying in your target heart rate range.

RECOVERY RATE

Periodically, retake your heart rate, using the six-second method, 30 seconds after you stop swimming, then again one minute after you stop. This will tell you how quickly your heart rate returns to normal. Rate of recovery is another indication of conditioning.

Weight, Size and Body Composition

Body weight can be an indication of improved fitness, if the swimmer has excess weight. However, for many swimmers, their body weight can actually increase slightly as they gain conditioning! This is not a cause for alarm. Rather, it is an indication that muscle is being built. As muscle is denser than fat, it weighs more. Once muscle is built, and used, you will actually burn more calories, as working muscles require more fuel.

But, instead of focusing only on body weight, focus on body size. The long muscles developed by swimmers tend to make the body and limbs more slender. For many people, it may be more satisfying to measure waist, hip and chest size rather than stand on a scale.

Probably the best body measurement to indicate fitness is a body composition test. This is a measurement of the body's fat content. While the ideal body fat content for the average adult male is considered to be 15%, and the average adult female is 22%, factors including age, frame, activity level and heredity must be taken into account. A health professional with a good understanding of your personal history is a good resource for this test. He or she will use one of several methods of measuring body fat index, including a skin caliper test, water displacement or electrical impedance. It should be noted that athletes with higher than normal muscle content must be measured carefully to get accurate results. While there are many gadgets available on the market to measure body fat, a visit to your health professional is advised for this purpose.

Cholesterol Balance
Many people who take up swimming achieve significant and quick results in terms of better cholesterol balance. Decreased bad cholesterol, increased good cholesterol level, as well as improved triglyceride levels have been recorded in as few as six weeks. Healthy cholesterol levels are a significant indication of fitness, and overall health, as they relate to risk factors for heart attack, stroke and cardiovascular disease. Measured through a blood test, healthy levels are defined as:

> LDL (Bad Cholesterol): Less than 200
> HDL (Good Cholesterol): More than 50
> Triglycerides (Fat): Less than 150

RECOVERY AND ADAPTATION

A Crucial Element of Success

An important and often overlooked element of achieving results in a fitness program is recovery between workouts. Resting is difficult for some of us! It is easy to get into the frame of mind that "more is better." To a certain extent, this is true. Pushing our bodies beyond the comfort level is necessary for improvement. This philosophy is bolstered by the rapid improvement some swimmers see when beginning a fitness routine. But for the most continuous results, both work and rest must be part of the training program. Finding the correct balance of work and rest is a not always easy. One size does not fit all. Coaches and swimmers who work together spend a great deal of time and energy designing the right balance of work and rest that enables the swimmer to achieve the best results.

As important as the quality, quantity and interval of the swimming one does, is the quality, quantity and interval of recovery periods. Rest between workouts is essential to allow the body to recover from the work it has done. This is the only way that improvement, or adaptation to a workload can be expected to occur over time. Without rest, the body can become fatigued, and further work only makes it more tired, instead of more fit.

If you are swimming on your own, advance planning of workout and recovery days is necessary. As a general rule, schedule at least two days off per week. As each person is different, your personal routine might include more rest days. You might design a weekly routine such as:

SWIM   SWIM   REST   SWIM   SWIM   REST   SWIM...

or

SWIM   REST   SWIM   REST   SWIM   REST   SWIM...

It is worth noting that when training multiple sports, that when a rest day from swimming is used as a workday for another sport, true rest is not really achieved. This has to be considered if the rate of adaptation and progress in swimming is not as swift as expected.

In order to continue a trend of improvement, rest is an essential ingredient of a fitness program.

SIGNS OF NON-ADAPTATION

It is important to be aware of the signs that you are not adapting to training. In a situation where a coach is not present to observe the swimmer's workouts, it is crucial that the swimmer remain alert to signs of non-adaptation, and actively make changes to stop this trend. Signs include:

FATIGUE EVEN AFTER REST

Being tired, especially in the early stages of a conditioning program is expected. However, if after several weeks of training that includes at least two days off per week, you are experiencing constant fatigue, that makes it difficult to enjoy or complete the workouts, or leaves you without the energy to carry on with your regular daily activities, then you need to make changes.
- Take additional rest days between workouts for a while
- Reduce the yardage of the workouts
- Work on stroke efficiency with swimming drills

CONSISTENT LACK OF IMPROVEMENT IN BENCHMARK SWIMS

During the course of doing the workouts in this collection, Benchmark Swims are called for periodically throughout the workouts. If you experience no improvement for three Benchmark Swims in a row, it can be an indication that you are too tired to exert. It can also point to a pattern of practicing swimming all of your workouts at medium speed, and never practicing going fast. If you are not seeing improvement in Benchmark Swims, you need to make changes.
- Take additional rest days between workouts for a while.
- Rest enough between sets, so you can do some 100% effort swimming at each workout.
- Reduce the yardage of the workouts.

SHOULDER PAIN

Any shoulder pain that is experienced during swimming should not be ignored! Shoulder pain can be an indication of "over use syndrome," or a technique problem. In either case, continuing the same training could very well worsen your condition, and you could find yourself unable to swim for an extended period of time. Shoulder pain means you need to make changes.

- Take several days off from swimming, or just kick your workouts.
- Have a coach check your stroke technique before resuming your training program.
- See a doctor if pain persists.
- Reduce the yardage of the workouts.

VALUING THE PROCESS

Observing improvements in your fitness is clearly rewarding, yet it may not happen every single time you measure your progress. This is natural. It is not the end of the world, and it is certainly not any indication that you should give up your pursuit of better swimming. Consider that swimming in and of itself is a rewarding experience. It is good for you on all levels: physically, mentally and emotionally. Give yourself credit for maintaining your swimming routine. Value the time you have to work things out in your head while you are swimming. Notice the smile on your face after you swim. Your swimming is time well spent. Enjoy every minute of it.

GETTING BACK ON THE HORSE

Shaping Up with swimming requires adopting a routine, and sticking with it. However, sometimes things come up. You could get the flu, the pool might be out of order, family responsibilities may come up. This is life.

The important thing is, if your routine is interrupted, don't give up... get back on the horse! Resume your training as soon as you can. Just as fitness takes time to build, it takes time to decline. The cumulative effect of the work that you have done will not be lost by a short disruption to your training routine. Keep going! Persevere!

GETTING STARTED

Preparing to Swim

Along with this book, you will need a few things to establish your Shape Up routine with swimming. These include:

A PLACE TO SWIM

Choose a pool that is convenient to you, so that maintaining your swimming routine will not be difficult, in terms of time and effort to get there. Especially in the beginning, and on low energy days, it is easy to find an excuse to skip your swimming workout. Making sure it is not a major effort just to get to the pool is a good first step.

The workouts in this book are formatted for a 25-yard/meter pool. If the pool you are swimming at is another length, for instance 50 meters, or 33.3 yards, the workouts and sets easily adapt to these pool lengths. You will have to recalculate yardage. If you are swimming workouts in two pools of different lengths, make sure you compare Benchmark Swims from the same pool length.

TIMING SYSTEM

This collection of workouts uses timed swims, timed rest, time intervals and heart rate measurements that require a clock. Many swim centers have large-faced pace clocks that are visible from the pool. You can also get a wristwatch that will perform the same functions, although some swimmers find it difficult to focus on the small numbers on a watch through their goggles during the brief rests between swims.

Whatever timing system you choose, think of the clock as your workout partner. It will keep you on schedule: telling you when to go, and how long to rest. It will give you feedback: telling you your times and reflecting your progress. The clock will be there with you. It will keep going as long as you swim. It will never lie!

EQUIPMENT

Besides a swim suit, a few other items you might need are:

- **Well-fitting Goggles**
  Good goggles really do make an extended time in the pool more enjoyable. Without the distraction of painful eyes and limited underwater vision, a swimmer can focus on their swimming experience.

- **A Kick Board**
  A kick board is not required, but some swimmers enjoy this face-up manner of accomplishing flutter and breaststroke kick. Kick boards should not be used for backstroke or dolphin kick as it detracts from good body position and kicking technique of these strokes. Figure 1 shows the correct and incorrect use of a kickboard.

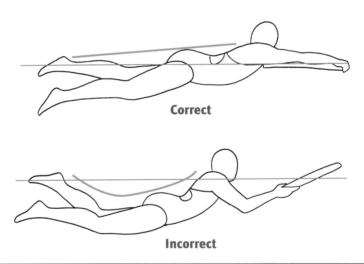

Correct

Incorrect

Figure 1
Position the kickboard against your chest, about at arm pit level, then rest your arms over the board. Balance your weight on the area where your chest meets the kickboard, so that the board is on the same plane as the water is sufrace. Avoid submerging the kickboard underwater. This will make you use your kick to stay up, rather tahn to move forward.

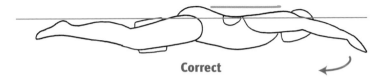

Correct

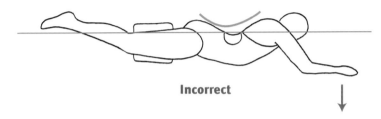

Incorrect

Figure 2
Use the smallest pull buoy possible, so that your legs do not float too high, distorting your body position, leading to reduced efficiency of your arm stroke. An over-size pull buoy can cause lower back pain.

- **A Pull Buoy**

A float worn between the legs during pulling sets, that allows the swimmer to maintain good body position without kicking. The smallest pull buoy possible should be used, just large enough to provide slight floatation for the stationary legs, but not enough to force the spine into a overly curved position. Figure 2 shows the correct and incorrect fit of a pull buoy.

- **A Plastic Bag**

Because it is best to have the workout you are doing at poolside, and to be able to easily refer to definitions and such, a zip type plastic bag for this book might be in order.

Workout Presentation

This collection of workouts is organized by stroke emphasis. The first 25 workouts focus on freestyle technique. The next 25 focus on backstroke technique, then 25 on breaststroke technique, and 25 on butterfly. It is important to be familiar with the presentation of the workouts to get the most benefit from them. This section describes the elements, terminology and formats used in this collection of workouts.

WORKOUT ELEMENTS

The workouts are built with various elements, each with its own purpose and relationship to the workout as a whole. These elements include:

Tip of the Day
The theme or emphasis of the workout, designed to focus the swimmer and his or her efforts during the workout.

Warm Up
The initial exercise period of sustained, medium intensity swimming lasting at least ten minutes, or at least 10% of your total yardage. Also an opportunity to review what you covered in your previous workout, and to refresh your "feel" for the water.

Kicking
Leg action only. A kick board is not necessary, but may be used for front flutter kick, or breaststroke kick. However, backstroke kick and dolphin kick should always be done without a kick board. Kicking is an excellent aerobic element of your workout.

Pulling
For freestyle only. Using a pull buoy to float your lower body, practice the upper body action of the stroke, including arm stroke, roll, alignment, use of core, stroke and breathing rhythm, leverage, cadence and body position. Many swimmers find pulling easier than swimming. This is an indication that time and attention should be paid to body position. These swimmers should use pulling as an

opportunity to analyze their body position, that is being "corrected" with the pull buoy, then try to duplicate that body position while swimming. Avoid using the pull buoy as a crutch when you are tired.

Stroke Drills

Exercises to emphasize one aspect of a stroke, or to practice a particular stroke element in order to maintain and build stroke efficiency and quality. Drills appear regularly within this collection of workouts, as a reminder of the importance of stroke quality. The following drills are called for by name within the workouts. Grouped by stroke, and in alphabetical order, each drill is accompanied here by a brief description of how to perform it, and its purpose. It is important to study the drills and understand how to do them correctly to get their full benefit. Most of these drills are also described in complete detail in the book *The 100 Best Swimming Drills*, also by Blythe Lucero. This is an excellent resource to accompany this collection of workouts. In addition to step-by-step descriptions, each drill is illustrated, and its purpose is clearly outlined. Feedback charts also follow each drill, to address common problems that can interfere with feeling the point of the drills.

FREESTYLE DRILLS

12 Kick Switch – To feel alignment, the rolling action of the stroke and the length of the stroke, kick on side for twelve kicks, low arm leading, other arm at your side, face in the water, then switch sides, and arm posi-tions, and repeat.

3 Strokes, 6 Kicks – To emphasize the rolling action of the stroke, and constant kicking, take three regular freestyle strokes with kicking, then kick only in the side floating position, low arm leading, other arm at your side, for six extra kicks, face in the water, then do three more freestyle strokes, then kick only floating on the other side for six extra kicks, and repeat.

All Thumbs Drill – Freestyle arm stroke extension actively pitching the wrist so the thumbs point in the direction you are swimming for better catch and stroke alignment (see illustration on next page).

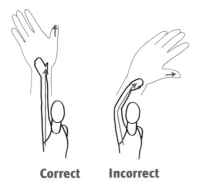

Correct   Incorrect

Figure 3
For the most aligned stroke, and the best catch, point forward, with your thumb in the direction you are going. Avoid over-reaching and leading your stroke off course with a collapsed wrist and elbow.

Catch Up – Like regular freestyle, except one arm catches up to the other in front, emphasizing that one arm should always be reaching, and the other stroking. Start with both arms leading, then do a complete freestyle stroke with one arm, when both arms are back in the leading position, do a freestyle stroke with the other arm, continue.

Freestyle with Dolphin – Regular freestyle arms with a dolphin kick, to practice coordinating the arm and leg actions. Each time your hand strikes the water in front, the feet snap down.

Hip Skating – Regular freestyle with an imaginary ice skate on each hip bone in front. Shift weight from hip to hip and achieve a skating rhythm to practice core leverage.

Pendulum – To feel leverage, switch rhythmically from one side floating position, with low are leading, and other arm in high elbow recovery position, to the other side, continue.

Push/Pull Freestyle – Regular freestyle isolating the pulling motion from full extension to the shoulder, and the pushing motion from the shoulder to the end of the stroke past the hip.

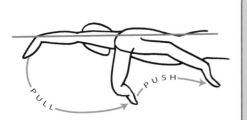

Figure 4
The path of the freestyle arm stroke underwater. Pull when your hand is in front of your shoulder. Push when it is behind or shoulder.

BACKSTROKE DRILLS

Armpit Lift – Exaggerating the roll of the backstroke to feel that the high recovering side provides leverage to the low stroking side of the body.

Backstroke 3 Strokes, 6 Kicks – To emphasize the rolling action of the stroke, and constant kicking, take three regular strokes with kicking, then kick only in the side floating position, low arm leading, other arm at your side, for six extra kicks, face out of the water, then do three more strokes, then kick only floating on the other side for six extra kicks, and repeat.

Backstroke 12 Kick Switch – To feel alignment, the rolling action, and the length of the stroke, kick on side for twelve kicks, low arm leading, other arm at your side, face up, then switch sides, and arm positions.

One Arm Pull/Push Backstroke – Single arm backstroke, with still arm at your side, trying to isolate the pulling motion from full extension to the shoulder, and the pushing motion from the shoulder to the end of the stroke past the hip.

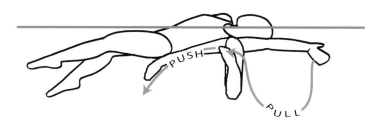

Figure 5
The path of the backstroke underwater. Pull when your hand is above your shoulder. Push wehn your hand is below your shoulder.

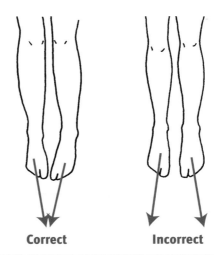

Correct   Incorrect

Figure 6
Position your feet pigeon toed for a stronger more unified kicking action. Without the pigeon toed foot position, the kick tend to be weaker and divided.

Pigeon Toed Kicking – Backstroke kicking with the feet and knees turned slightly inward to a pigeon toed position to achieve a larger foot surface to push water upward, and less drag from knees breaking the surface.

Rhythmic Breathing – Practicing patterns of breathing in backstroke, including inhale on one stroke, exhale on the other, inhale and exhale during each recovery, and, inhale during one stroke cycle, and exhale on the next, in order to actively develop rhythmic breathing in backstroke.

Roll, Pull/Roll, Push – Regular backstroke feeling that the continuous rolling action provides momentum and leverage to the pull and the push of the arm stroke. Roll down to catch and pull, roll up to transition and push.

Up and Over – Practicing the path of the backstroke arm stroke, do regular backstroke, focusing on the arm stroke as you catch deep, then move your hand up and over your stationary elbow, then press the hand past the hip.

BREASTSTROKE DRILLS

3 Kick Breaststroke – To emphasize that each stroke begins and ends in a streamline position, float in a hand lead position and do three breaststroke kicks in a row, then do one complete stroke cycle of arm stroke, breathing, kick and glide, and repeat.

Breaststroke Alternating Dolphin and Breaststroke Kick – One breast-stroke arm stroke with a dolphin as you press out, and another as you sweep in, then a complete breaststroke arm stroke, breath, kick and glide. Repeat alternating strokes to emphasize the rocking action and core use in the breaststroke.

Breaststroke with Dolphin – Breaststroke arm stroke with a dolphin as you press out, and another as you sweep in, emphasizing the rocking action and core use in the breaststroke.

Corners Drill – Regular breast-stroke, focusing on achieving lift for the breathing without pressing down on the water, but instead, by accelerating from the outsweep into the insweep, and holding on to the water during the transition from one to the other.

Eyes on the Water – Regular breaststroke where you look down at the water while inhaling, rather than forward, maintaining a constant chin position through-out the stroke in order to con-tinue the forward line of the stroke, and maximize leverage.

Figure 7
Hold on to the water at the corners. As you change from outsweep to insweep accelerate your arm stroke.

Hand Speed Drill – To practice no pauses in the arm stroke, especially at the "drag point" that can occur at the transition from in sweep and recovery, do breaststroke arm stroke with flutter kick, trying to accomplish a complete arm stroke (out sweep, in sweep, recovery) within the time it takes to do four flutter kick downbeats, then hold in streamline for six kicks, and continue.

Shoot to Streamline – Regular breaststroke where you focus on accelerating through the drag point of the stroke, just after the in sweep, and use the momentum to get back to the streamline position.

Stroke Up to Breathe, Kick Down to Glide – Regular breaststroke focusing on stroking and breathing while rocking up, and kicking while rocking down, to emphasize available stroke leverage.

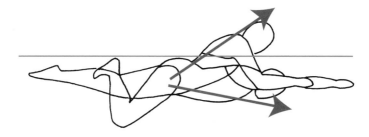

Figure 8
With the hips as your center of balance, stroke up to breathe, kick down to glide.

Thread the Needle – Regular breaststroke where as you approach recovery you try to make a small hole in the water with your hands, then pass through that same hole with your elbows, shoulders and head, chest, hips, legs and feet, to feel the most streamlined stroke.

BUTTERFLY DRILLS

Advanced One Arm Butterfly – From a head leading position, do butterfly with one arm only, while the other arm remains at your side, to practice butterfly stroke rhythm in a more sustainable manner than the full stroke. Also emphasizes the pull and push of the arm stroke, and getting the chest down when the arm is forward.

Chest Balance – Regular butterfly focusing on the point when your chest is at its lowest point, and you feel as if you are riding downhill and forward for an instant before you start your arm stroke and your chest rises, giving leverage to the stroke that would not be present from a flat body position.

Figure 9
Balance your chest as you reach to your catch. Feel that your chest is lower than your hips at this instant.

Coordination Checkpoint – Regular butterfly focusing on coordinating three actions so they occur at exactly the same time: the round off finish of the underwater arm stroke, the downward snap of the second kick, and the end of the inhale.

Hammer and Nail – Regular butterfly, breathing each stroke, imagining that your forehead is a hammer and the water is a nail. When your head returns to the water, powered by your upper body, strike the nail with force. Avoid striking the water with your chin, which will lead to frontal drag and poor body position.

Left Arm, Right Arm, Both Arms – From a hand leading position, do one butterfly stroke with your left arm only, then one with your right arm, then a stroke with both arms. Start each new stroke when the previous stroke returns to the starting point. To practice butterfly stroke rhythm, and to bridge from drill to swim.

One Arm Butterfly – From a hand leading position, do butterfly with one arm only, while the other arm remains extended, to practice butterfly stroke rhythm in a more sustainable manner than the full stroke. Also emphasizes the pull and push of the arm stroke, and keeping the hips up.

Pinkies Up – Regular butterfly focusing on maintaining a consistent "pinkie up" hand position during recovery, so the elbows do not drag through the water, but rather the arms make a unified and strong arch over the water's surface.

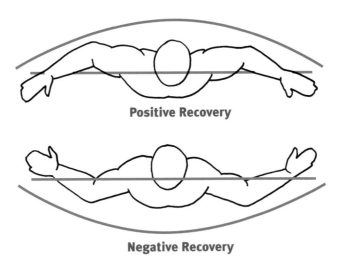

Positive Recovery

Negative Recovery

Figure 10
Achieve a positive recovery. Swing your arms over the water with your pinkies up. If you recover thumbs up, your elbows will drag through the water, and slow you down.

Reaching to a "Y" – Regular butterfly focusing on a wide "Y"-shaped entry, leading with the thumbs in order to produce the most aligned position to start the stroke, and the best catch.

The Flop – Regular butterfly focusing on initiating the recovery from the shoulders to achieve a relaxed forward-reaching recovery. Release the water, pinkies up, swing arms wide and around from the shoulders, not the hands, until your arms are at shoulder level. Then, roll your shoulders forward and redirect your hands to reach forward, and as they do drop your chest into the water.

Timed Distance Swims

Swim continuously for a pre-set number of minutes, and count how many yards/meters are accomplished during that time. In this collection of workouts, distance swims of 5, 10 and 15 minutes are called for several times. These results should be recorded, like benchmark swims, and compared over time to track progress.

Speed Play

One of the oldest and most effective conditioning activities, also used in the training of runners and other athletes. In swimming, Speed Play calls for continuous swimming of a pre-set distance, with alternating periods of hard and easy effort. The easy effort period serves as recovery or "active rest" for the swimmer.

Interval Training

A widely used training method that is used to build endurance, pace and general swimming capacity. An interval set consists of multiple repetitions of a particular distance, which are accomplished on a pre-set time interval. The time interval encompasses the swim time plus rest time. While it would seem that the multiple short swims that commonly make up an interval set would make this a speed training activity, the fact that the rest between swims is usually too brief to recover enough to keep swimming intensity at a very high level makes the activity an endurance builder, rather than a speed builder. Interval training can be designed in several ways, including:

DESCENDING SETS

Swim each repeat slightly faster than the previous one, so that the swimming time of each repeat "descends." NOTE: False success can easily be achieved through a strategy that has the swimmer do the first repeat TOO slowly. When this is done, the first, or even first several repetitions are "throw away" swims, offering little value to the training. It is therefore important to take on the challenge to make EACH repeat count. A descending set that starts at a normal training intensity, and descends from that point is more beneficial. A "narrow descend," or only a slight increase in speed from one repeat to the next should be the goal. A "wide descend," or several seconds difference between one repeat and the next may indicate that the starting point was too slow. Keep in mind that while the times of each repeat should descend, the effort throughout the set should "ascend."

PACE SETS

Swimming each repeat at an even pace. Pace sets are excellent for training for distance swimming, as they allow the swimmer to train at a faster pace than they could maintain without the minor rest breaks between repeats. The goal is that the swimmer will be able to "feel" the pace that they need to hold when they swim their continuous distance swim. Once again, the starting time will determine the effectiveness of the set. If it is easy to make it all the way through the set, then the starting time is too slow. It should be a real challenge to complete the last few repeats in the same time as the beginning ones.

DESCENDING INTERVAL SETS

Swimming repeats with reducing rest after each one. Very difficult! This simulates the conditions in a race where more and more effort is required to maintain one's rate of swimming, as less and less oxygen replenishes the muscles. Descending interval sets can also be done where one interval is maintained for a number of repeats, then decreased, either once or a number of times.

Stroke Contrasts

Alternating distances of two different strokes to compare and contrast stroke elements, including body position, rhythm, catch, kick, coordination, breathing and cadence. An excellent way to improve a weaker stroke is by studying what makes a stronger stroke work, and employing those observations in the weaker stroke. Based on certain key stroke similarities, good stroke contrasts include:

Freestyle / Backstroke
Freestyle / Butterfly
Butterfly / Breaststroke

Sprint Sets

Sets calling for high effort, high velocity, intense swimming for a short distance. Sprinting is a valuable activity for building fast twitch muscle, and to observe how stroke quality works at a faster rate than normal training speed. Sprint sets require more rest than endurance-based sets to enable the body to exert at the highest level possible several times.

Benchmark Swims

A timed swim at 100% effort, or "race pace" to be recorded and compared to other benchmark swims done at other workouts, in order to track progress.

Cool Down

The final exercise period of easy, continuous swimming that is important to gradually return the heart to its regular rhythm, and rinse out the muscles. These workouts call for a cool down of 200 yards. This is a minimum. More easy swimming at the end of your workout is encouraged.

WORKOUT TERMINOLOGY

It will be important to be familiar with the following terms and swimming jargon used throughout this collection of workouts, appearing here in alphabetical order:

- **5 Minute Swim:**
  Swimming as far as possible within a 5 minute time limit.

- **10 Minute Swim:**
  Swimming as far as possible within a 10 minute time limit.

- **15 Minute Swim:**
  Swimming as far as possible within a 15 minute time limit.

- **25, 50, 75, 100, 200:**
  Refers to the distance to be done in terms of a 25 yard/meter pool. A 25 would be one length, a 50 would be two lengths, a 100 would be four lengths, etc.

- **4 x 25:**
  Refers to the number of times a distance is to be done, for instance, in this example, 25 yards will be done four times.

- **50 Easy:**
  A short recovery swim, and a chance to reflect on the set that you just finished.

- **Alternating 25s (or 50s) of:**
  calls for switching between two activities after a specific distance.

- **Benchmark Swim:**
  A timed swim at 100% effort that should be recorded and compared with other Benchmark Swims over time in order to track progress.

- **Breaststroke Kick:**
  The kick done with the breaststroke, using a simultaneous, mirror image circular rotation of the legs. The breaststroke kick is done completely underwater, using the bottoms of the feet to push water.

- **Build:**
  Increasing speed throughout a swim, from stroke to stroke steadily throughout the distance.

- **Count strokes:**
  Counting the total number of strokes it takes per length of the pool

- **Descending:**
  Swimming each repeat in a series slightly faster than the previous one, so that the times "descend."

- **Dolphin:**
  The head to toe body wave action done with butterfly. Often referred to as a kick, the legs move together, but as a result of the action initiated high in the body.

- **Drill/Swim:**
  An exercise that alternates drill and swim, in order to incorporate the skills emphasized in the drill into the full swimming stroke.

- **Fast/Easy:**
  Alternating high effort and fast stroke tempo, and easy effort and slower stroke tempo.

- **Flutter Kick:**
  The kick done with Freestyle and Backstroke, using an alternating leg action.

- **Hands leading:**
  A drill or kick position with the arms extended over the head, so the hands lead the way through the water.

- **Head leading:**
  A drill or kick position with the arms positioned at the sides of the body, so the head leads the way through the water.

- **Interval:**
  The time that each repeat in a set will be started on. The interval includes the swim and the rest time.

- **Kick –**
  other than breaststroke kick: Any kick other than breaststroke kick. The reason for this is that breaststroke kick should only be done when the knees are completely warmed up to avoid injury.

- **Leg Burners:**
  All out sprint kicking using flutter kick.

- **On your interval:**
  Maintaining a constant time interval for each repeat in a set that includes both swim and rest time. For 50s or 100s, the interval is usually preset by adding 10-15 seconds to the first swim time.

- **Pace:** Holding steady times.

- **Pyramid:**
  A kind of set that consists of swims that increase in distance to a peak, then follow the same pattern in reverse. For example: 25, 50, 75, 100, 75, 50, 25.

- **THR:** Target Heart Rate

- **w/15 SR:**
  Refers to the amount of rest (R) in seconds (S) between swims. For example, in this case: with 15 seconds rest.

- **Your choice:**
  Swimmer chooses the stroke or drill.

WORKOUT FORMAT

Each workout begins with a Tip of the Day, and ends with the total yardage. Tips of the Day are designed to orient the swimmer to the theme, or goal of the workout. Total yardage is included as one measure of fitness. All of the workouts in this book total between 2,200 and 3,500 yards/meters. Workout content is presented in a sequential format, one activity after the other, using a standardized set of directions. Each activity or set appears as a string of commands.

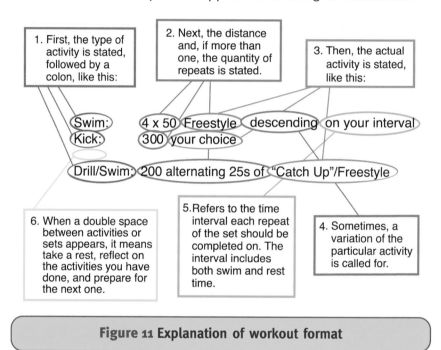

Figure 11 Explanation of workout format

Swimmer's Progress Log

Measuring your progress periodically gives you clear feedback. Even if you are not training for a competitive event, timing yourself, and tracking your progress is worthwhile in terms of keeping you motivated to stay with your Shape Up program. The following pages provide the framework for you to record your progress, and celebrate it along the way.

TIMED SWIMS

FREESTYLE

Date	50 yards	100 yards	200 yards	500 yards	1 mile

BACKSTROKE

Date	50 yards	100 yards	200 yards

BREASTSTROKE

Date	50 yards	100 yards	200 yards

BUTTERFLY

Date	25 yards	50 yards	100 yards

INTERVAL SETS

FREESTYLE

10 x 50				5 x 100			
Date	Type*	Swim Times	Interval	Date	Type*	Swim Times	Interval

BACKSTROKE

10 x 50				5 x 100			
Date	Type*	Swim Times	Interval	Date	Type*	Swim Times	Interval

BREASTSTROKE

10 x 50				5 x 100			
Date	Type*	Swim Times	Interval	Date	Type*	Swim Times	Interval

BUTTERFLY

8 x 25				8 x 50			
Date	Type*	Swim Times	Interval	Date	Type*	Swim Times	Interval

*Type refers to Descending, Pace, or Descending Interval

DISTANCE SWIMS

Date	5 minute Swim	10 minute Swim	15 minute Swim

WORKOUTS

Date	Total Yardage	Workout Duration	Notes

WORKOUTS (continuted)

Date	Total Yardage	Workout Duration	Notes

RESTING HEARTRATE

Date	Heartrate

TARGET HEART RATE

Date	THR	Duration

BODY WEIGHT

Date	Weight

SIZE

Date	Waist	Chest	Hips

BODY COMPOSITION

Date	% of Body Fat

CHOLESTEROL

Date	Bad	Good	Triglycerides

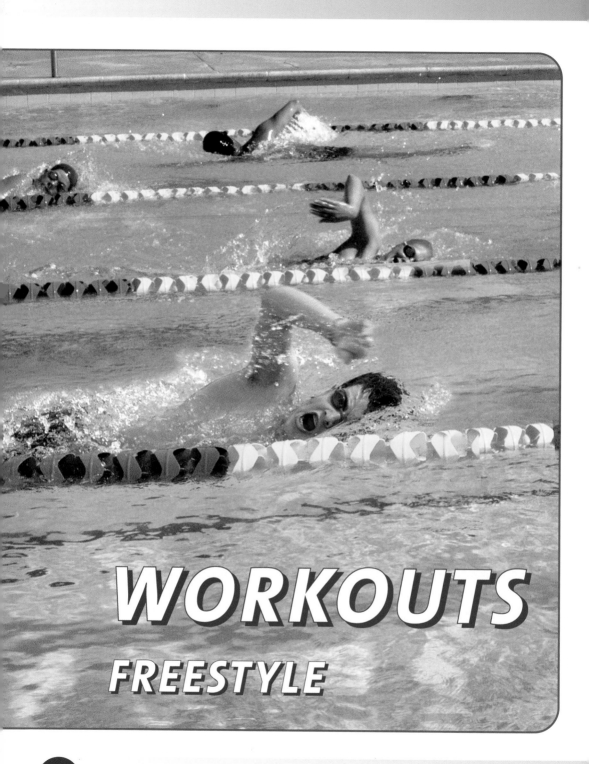

WORKOUTS
FREESTYLE

Workouts for Freestyle

1 Workout

Tip of the Day: Feel the difference between fast and easy effort.

Warm up:	400
Kick:	200 Flutter Kick
Drill:	200 alternating 25s of "Catch Up"/Freestyle w/10 SR
Swim:	8 x 50 Freestyle – Fast/Easy w/15 SR
50 Easy	
Pull:	300
Kick:	200 Flutter Kick – Fast/Easy
Benchmark Swim:	50 Freestyle for time
50 Easy	
Swim:	6 x 25 Freestyle – Fast/Easy w/ 30 SR
Cool down:	200
Total:	2,200

2 Workout

Tip of the Day: Establish your interval by timing your first repeat of the series and adding 15 seconds rest. Maintain this interval for the whole set.

Warm up:	400
Kick:	300 Flutter Kick
Drill:	200 "12 Kick Switch"
Swim:	100 Freestyle
Swim:	6 x 50 Freestyle on your interval
Kick:	200
Swim:	8 x 50 Freestyle on your interval
Benchmark Swim:	100 Freestyle
Cool down:	200
Total:	2,200

3Workout

Tip of the Day: Try to maintain a constant stroke count.

Warm up:	400
Drill:	100 "3 Strokes/6 Kicks"
Kick:	100 Flutter Kick
Drill:	100 "Catch Up"
Kick:	100 Flutter Kick
Swim:	4 x 50 Freestyle on your interval
Pull:	200
Swim:	4 x 50 Freestyle on your interval
50 Easy	
Benchmark Swim:	200 Freestyle
50 Easy	
Swim/Kick:	10 x 50 alternating Freestyle/Flutter Kick with 15 SR
Cool down:	200
Total:	2,300

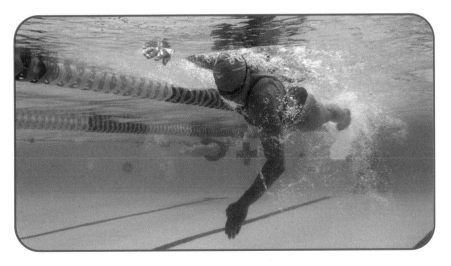

4Workout

Tip of the Day: Establish your interval for 100. Your rest after 100 should be 15-20 seconds.

Warm up:	400
Kick:	200 Flutter Kick
Drill/Swim:	200 "3 Strokes/6 Kicks"/Freestyle
Swim:	3 x 100 Freestyle on your interval
50 Easy	
Swim:	4 x 100 Freestyle on your interval
50 Easy	
Swim:	5 x 100 Freestyle on your interval
Cool down:	200
Total:	2,300

5Workout

Tip of the Day: When you get tired, roll in and out of your stroke more. Keep your strokes long.

Warm up:	400
Kick:	8 x 25 Flutter Kick w/10 SR
Drill:	100 "Hip Skating"
Swim:	500 Freestyle
Pull:	400
Swim:	300 Freestyle
Pull:	200
Swim:	100
Cool down:	200
Total:	2,400

6 Workout

Tip of the Day: Focus on your stroke rhythm.

Warm up:	400
Kick:	4 x 50 Flutter Kick w/10 SR
Drill:	100 "Pendulum"
Swim:	8 x 50 Freestyle – descending, on your interval
Pull:	300
Swim:	4 x 100 Freestyle – descending, on your interval
50 Easy	
Benchmark Swim:	50 Freestyle
50 Easy	
Kick:	200 Flutter Kick
50 Easy	

Timed Distance Swim: 5-Minute Swim

Cool down:	200
Total:	2,400 + 5-Minute Swim

7 Workout

Tip of the Day: Work on establishing an even pace.

Warm up:	400
Kick:	200 Flutter Kick
Drill:	100 "Pull/Push Freestyle"
Swim:	8 x 25 – Build w/15 SR
Swim:	6 x 50 Freestyle – descending, on your interval
Swim:	10 x 50 Freestyle – pace, on your interval
Pull:	500
Benchmark Swim:	100 Freestyle
Cool down:	200
Total:	2,500

8Workout

Tip of the Day: Think of a longer swim as several short swims stuck together.

Warm up:	400
Kick:	200 Flutter Kick
Swim:	8 x 25 Build w/15 SR
Swim:	6 x 100 – 10 SR after odd 100s,
	20 SR after even 100s
Swim:	3 x 200 Freestyle – descending w/20 SR
Benchmark Swim:	200 Freestyle
Cool Down:	200
Total:	2,600

9Workout

Tip of the Day: Stay within target heart rate range.

Warm up:	400
Kick:	200 Flutter Kick
Swim:	4 x 100 Freestyle – descending, on your interval
Swim:	5 x 100 Freestyle – pace, on your interval
Pull:	400
Benchmark Swim:	500 Freestyle
Cool down:	200
Total:	2,600

Workout

Tip of the Day: Stay focused on stroke quality and pace.

Warm up:	400
Kick:	6 x 50 Flutter Kick w/10 SR
Benchmark Swim:	1 mile (72 lengths in a 25 yd. pool)
Cool down:	200
Total:	2,700

11 **Workout**

Tip of the Day: Learn to change speeds both gradually (build), and suddenly (fast/easy).

Warm up:	400
Kick:	300 Flutter Kick – alternating Fast/Easy
Drill/Swim:	200 "All Thumbs Drill"/Freestyle
Swim:	8 x 50 Freestyle – Build, on your interval
Pull:	400
Swim:	8 x 50 Freestyle – Build, on your interval
Benchmark Swim:	50 Freestyle
50 Easy	
200 Kick	
Swim:	8 x 25 Freestyle alternating Fast/Easy w/30 SR
Cool down:	200
Total:	2,800

# Workout 12

Tip of the Day: Try reducing your interval by 5 seconds.

Warm up:	400
Kick:	200 Flutter Kick
Drill/Swim:	200 "Freestyle with Dolphin"/Freestyle
Swim:	4 x 50 Freestyle – Pace, on your new interval
Pull:	200
Swim:	6 x 50 Freestyle – Pace, on your new interval
Pull:	200
Swim:	8 x 50 Freestyle – Pace, on your new interval
Kick:	200
50 Easy	
Benchmark Swim:	100 Freestyle
50 Easy	
Kick:	4 x 25 Leg Burners, w/15 SR
Cool down:	200
Total:	2,800

Workout

Tip of the Day: Find your stride.

Warm up:	400
Kick:	4 x 50 Flutter Kick w/10 SR
Drill:	200 "Pendulum"
Drill:	200 "Hip Skating"

Swim:	10 x 50 – Build, on your interval
Swim:	5 x 100 Descending, on your interval

50 Easy

Timed Distance Swim: 10-Minute Swim

50 Easy

Kick:	200 Flutter Kick

Swim:	8 x 25 Fast/Easy w/15 SR
Kick:	8 x 25 Leg Burners w/15 SR

Cool down:	200

Total:	2,900

14 Workout

Tip of the Day: Try maintaining your 100 time with less rest.

Warm up:	400
Kick:	200 Flutter Kick
Drill:	200 – your choice
Swim:	4 x 50 Freestyle – Build, on your interval
Kick:	4 x 25 Leg Burners w/15 SR
Pull:	500
Swim:	5 x 100 Freestyle – Pace, on your interval
Swim:	4 x 100 Freestyle – Pace, on your interval minus 5 seconds
Swim:	3 x 100 Freestyle – Pace, on your interval minus 10 seconds
Cool down:	200
Total:	3,000

15 Workout

Tip of the Day: Keep your kick in rhythm with your stroke.

Warm up:	400
Kick:	8 x 50 Flutter Kick w/10 SR
Drill:	200 "3 Strokes/6 Kicks"
Swim:	12 x 25 Freestyle – Build w/10 SR
Swim:	8 x 50 Freestyle – Pace, on your interval
Swim:	5 x 100 Freestyle – Descending, on your interval
Pull:	3 x 200 w/20 SR

Timed Distance Swim: 15-Minute Swim

Cool down:	200
Total:	3,000 + 15-Minute Swim

Workout

Tip of the Day: Hold on to the water as you increase the rate of your stroke.

Warm up:	400
Kick:	8 x 50 Flutter Kick – Fast/Easy w/10 SR
Drill:	200 "Push/Pull Freestyle"
Swim:	10 x 50 – Build, on your interval
Pull:	300
Swim:	8 x 50 – Pace, on your interval
Pull:	300
Swim:	6 x 50 Descending, on your interval
Benchmark Swim:	50 Freestyle
50 Easy	
Benchmark Swim:	50 Freestyle
Cool down:	200
Total:	3,250

17 Workout

Tip of the Day: Are you staying within target heart rate range?

Warm up:	400
Kick:	6 x 50 Flutter Kick – Build w/10 SR
Drill/Swim:	6 x 50 – alternating 50s of your choice Drill/ Freestyle
Swim:	10 x 50 – Pace, on your interval
Swim:	5 x 100 – Pace, on your interval
Pull:	500
Kick:	200 Flutter Kick
Benchmark Swim:	100 Freestyle
50 Easy	
Swim:	12 x 25 Freestyle – Fast/Fast/Easy... w/15 SR
Cool down:	200
Total:	3,350

18 Workout

Tip of the Day: Focus on stroke rhythm, range and relaxation.

Warm up:	400
Kick:	300 Flutter Kick – every third length fast
Drill:	200 "3 Strokes, 6 Kicks"
Drill/Swim:	300 "3 Strokes, 6 Kicks"/Freestyle
Swim:	4 x 50 Freestyle – Build, on your interval
Swim:	4 x 50 Freestyle – Descending, on your interval
Swim:	4 x 50 Freestyle – Pace, on your interval
Kick:	200 Flutter Kick
Pull:	200
Benchmark Swim:	200 Freestyle
50 Easy	
Kick:	200 Flutter Kick
Pull:	200
Swim/Kick:	12 x 25 – alternating 25s of Fast Swim/Leg Burner w/15 SR
Cool down:	200
Total:	3,350

Workout

Tip of the Day: Pace your 100s.

Warm up:	400
Kick:	100 Flutter Kick
Drill/Swim:	200 – your choice/Freestyle
Kick:	100 Flutter Kick
Swim:	3 x 100 Freestyle on your interval
Swim:	4 x 100 Freestyle on your interval minus 5 seconds
Swim:	5 x 100 Freestyle on your interval minus 10 seconds
Pull:	500
Benchmark Swim:	500 Freestyle
50 Easy	
Kick:	8 x 25 Flutter Kick – Leg Burner/Easy w/15 SR
Cool down:	200
Total:	3,450

Workout

Tip of the Day: Pace by 50s.

Warm up:	400
Kick/Swim:	8 x 50 – alternating 50s of Kick and Swim w/10 SR
Swim:	8 x 50 – Descending, on your interval
Kick:	300 flutter kick
Benchmark Swim:	1 mile Freestyle
Cool down:	200
Total:	3,500

21 **Workout**

Tip of the Day: Use your core to power your stroke.

Warm up:	400
Kick:	300 Flutter Kick – alternating Fast/Easy
Drill:	200 "3 Strokes/6 Kicks"
Drill:	200 "Hip Skating"

Swim:	10 x 50 Freestyle – Build, on your interval
Swim:	5 x 100 Freestyle – Descending, on your interval
Pull:	500

Timed Distance Swim: 5-Minute Swim
50 Easy
Kick: 200 Flutter Kick

Benchmark Swim: 50 Freestyle

Kick:	200 Flutter Kick
Swim:	8 x 25 Freestyle – alternating Fast/Easy w/15 SR

Cool down: 200

Total: 3,500 + 5-Minute Swim

Workout

Tip of the Day: In 100, build through the first 50, then power through the second 50.

Warm up:	400
Kick:	8 x 25 Flutter Kick w/10 SR
Drill/Swim:	200 "Freestyle with Dolphin"/Freestyle
Drill/Swim:	200 "Catch Up"/Freestyle
Swim:	10 x 50 – Build, on your interval
Kick:	200 Flutter Kick
Swim:	5 x 100 – Descending, on your interval
Kick:	200 Flutter Kick
Benchmark Swim:	100 Freestyle
Swim/Pull:	4 x 200 – alternating 200s of Pull/Swim w/20 SR
Cool down:	200
Total:	3,500

Workout

Tip of the Day: Maintain your "feel" of the water.

Warm up:	400
Kick:	200 Flutter Kick
Drill:	200 your choice
Swim:	4 x 50 Freestyle – Build, on your interval
Swim:	4 x 50 – Descending, on your interval
Swim:	2 x 100 Freestyle – Build, on your interval
Swim:	2 x 100 Freestyle – Pace, on your interval
Swim:	100, 15 SR, 2 x 50 w/10 SR
50 Easy	
Benchmark Swim:	200 Freestyle
50 Easy	
Kick:	200 Flutter Kick
Timed Distance Swim:	10-Minute Swim
Cool down:	200
Total:	3,500 + 10-Minute Swim

Workout

Tip of the Day: Establish your pace, then hold on to it!

Warm up:	400
Kick:	200 Flutter Kick
Drill:	100 "Catch Up"
Drill:	100 "All Thumbs Drill"
Drill:	100 "Pendulum"
Swim:	10 x 50 Freestyle – Pace, on your interval
Pull:	500
Swim:	5 x 100 Freestyle – Pace, on your interval
Kick:	200 Flutter Kick
Benchmark Swim:	500 Freestyle
50 Easy	
Kick:	6 x 25 Leg Burners w/10 SR
Cool down:	200
Total:	3,500

Workout

Tip of the Day: Swim within your target heart rate range.

Warm up:	400
Kick:	200 Flutter Kick
Drill/Swim:	300 "Catch Up"/Freestyle

Swim:	5 x 100 Freestyle – Pace, on your interval
Pull:	500
Swim:	20 x 50 – Pace, on your interval

Timed Distance Swim: 15-Minute Swim

Swim:	100 Freestyle
Kick:	4 x 25 Leg Burners w/15 SR
Swim:	100 Freestyle
Kick:	4 x 25 Leg Burners w/15 SR

Cool down:	200

Total:	3,500

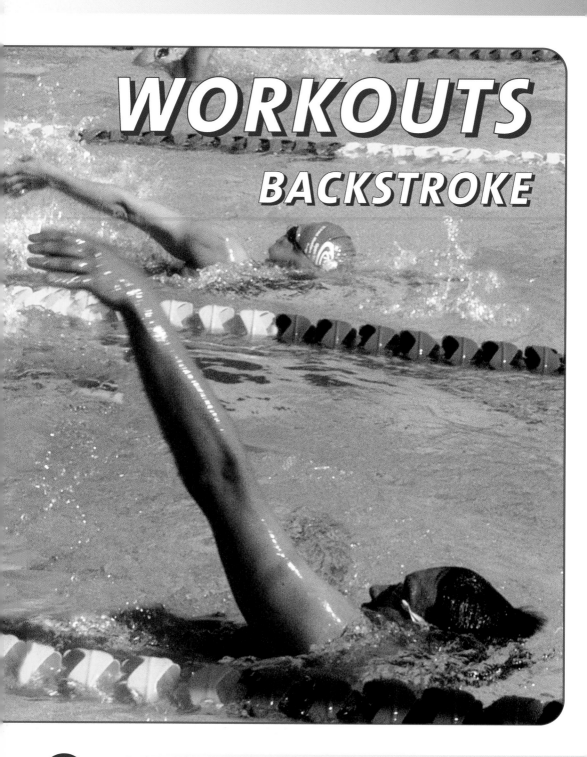

WORKOUTS

BACKSTROKE

Shape Up Workouts for Backstroke

26 Workout

Tip of the Day: Compare and contrast Backstroke and Freestyle.

Warm up:	400
Kick:	8 x 25 alternating on front/on back w/10 SR – hands leading
Drill:	200 alternating 25s of "Freestyle 12 Kick Switch"/ "Backstroke 12 Kick Switch"
Drill/Swim:	200 "Backstroke 12 Kick Switch"/Backstroke
Swim:	4 x 100 alternating 25s of Freestyle/Backstroke w/15 SR
Swim:	8 x 50 alternating 50 Freestyle/50 Backstroke w/15 SR
50 Easy	
Kick:	100 your choice
Benchmark Swim:	50 Backstroke
Cool down:	200
Total:	2,200

Workout

Tip of the Day: Establish your Backstroke interval for 50s.

Warm up:	400
Kick:	200 alternating 25s on front/back
Drill:	200 "One Arm Pull/Push Backstroke" – alternate 25 left arm/25 right arm
Swim:	200 – alternating 25s of Freestyle and Backstroke
Swim:	4 x 50 Backstroke – on your interval
Pull:	300
Swim:	10 x 50 Backstroke – on your interval
Cool down:	200
Total:	2,200

Workout

Tip of the Day: Set your stroke rhythm to your breathing rhythm.

Warm up:	400
Kick:	200 your choice
Drill:	4 x 50 "Rhythmic Breathing" w/10 SR
Drill:	200 "3 Strokes/6 Kicks"
Swim:	10 x 50 alternating lengths of Freestyle/Backstroke w/15 SR
Pull:	300
Benchmark Swim:	100 Backstroke
Kick:	8 x 25 Flutter Kick on back, hands leading w/10 SR
Cool down:	100
Total:	2,200

Workout

Tip of the Day: Establish your Backstroke interval for 100s.

Warm up:	400
Kick:	200 Flutter Kick on back, hands leading
Drill:	4 x 50 "Backstroke 12 Kick Switch" w/15 SR
Drill:	4 x 50 "3 Strokes/6 Kicks Backstroke" w/15 SR
Swim:	200 alternating 25s of Freestyle/Backstroke
Swim:	5 x 100 Backstroke on your interval
Pull:	200
Swim:	8 x 25 alternating 25s of Backstroke/Freestyle w/15 SR
Cool down:	200
Total:	2,300

Workout 30

Tip of the Day: Maintain a constant stroke count.

Warm up:	200
Kick:	4 x 50 Flutter Kick w/10 SR
Kick:	4 x 50 Flutter Kick on back w/10 SR
Drill:	4 x 50 "Backstroke 12 Kick Switch" w/15 SR
Drill:	4 x 50 "One Arm Pull/Push Backstroke" w/15 SR
Swim:	4 x 50 Backstroke on your interval – count strokes per length
Swim:	2 x 100 Backstroke on your interval – count strokes per length
Benchmark Swim:	200 Backstroke
50 Easy	
Pull:	300 Pull
Kick:	200 your choice
Swim:	8 x 25 alternating 25s Backstroke/ Freestyle w/15 SR
Cool down:	100
Total:	2,450

Workout

Tip of the Day: Hold on to the water, but increase your stroke rate.

Warm up:	400
Kick:	200 your choice
Drill:	4 x 50 "Backstroke 3 Strokes/6 Kicks" w/10 SR
Swim:	4 x 25 Backstroke w/10 SR
Drill:	4 x 50 "Up and Over" w/10 SR
Swim:	4 x 25 Backstroke w/10 SR

500 Pull

4 x 50 Backstroke – Descending, on your interval

4 x 50 Freestyle – Descending, on your interval

Benchmark Swim: 50 Backstroke

50 Easy

Kick: 4 x 25 Flutter Kick on your back – arms leading w/10 SR

Cool down: 200

Total: 2,500

Workout

Tip of the Day: Do six quick kicks for each arm cycle.

Warm up:	400
Kick:	200 your choice
Drill:	4 x 25 "Pigeon Toed Kicking" w/10 SR
Drill:	200 "3 Strokes/6 Kicks"
Swim:	10 x 50 Freestyle on your interval
Swim:	10 x 50 Backstroke on your interval
Pull:	200
Swim:	8 x 25 alternating Freestyle/Backstroke w/15 SR
Cool down:	200
Total:	2,500

33 Workout

Tip of the Day: Develop good foot position.

Warm up:	400
Kick:	200 your choice
Drill:	200 "One Arm Pull/Push Backstroke"
Drill:	200 "Roll, Pull/Roll, Push"
Swim:	4 x 200 alternating 200s of Freestyle and Backstroke w/20 SR
Pull:	500
Benchmark Swim:	100 Backstroke
Cool down:	200
Total:	2,600

34 **Workout**

Tip of the Day: Check target heart rate.

Warm up:	400
Kick:	200 Flutter Kick
Kick:	4 x 25 Flutter Kick on back w/10 SR
Drill:	200 "Armpit Lift"
Drill/Swim:	200 "Armpit Lift"/Backstroke
Swim:	200 Backstroke
Swim:	5 x 100 Freestyle on your interval
Swim:	5 x 100 Backstroke on your interval
Swim:	4 x 25 Fast Backstroke w/30 SR
Cool down:	200
Total:	2,600

Workout

Tip of the Day: Roll in and out of each stroke.

Warm up:	400
Kick:	300 Flutter Kick – alternating 25s on back/on front
Drill:	200 "One Arm Pull/Push Backstroke"
Drill/Swim:	200 "3 Strokes/6 Kicks Backstroke"/Backstroke
Swim:	4 x 50 Backstroke – Descending, on your interval
Swim:	200 Backstroke
Swim:	4 x 50 Freestyle – Descending, on your interval
Swim:	200 Freestyle
Kick/Swim:	300 – your choice
Benchmark Swim:	200 Backstroke
Cool down:	200
Total:	2,600

36 Workout

Tip of the Day: Accelerate your stroke from start to finish.

Warm up:	400
Kick:	6 x 50 Flutter Kick – alternating 50s on front/on back
Drill/Swim:	10 x 50 alternating 25s of "One Arm Pull/Push Backstroke"/Backstroke
Swim:	200 Backstroke
Swim:	150 Backstroke
Swim:	100 Backstroke
Swim:	50 Backstroke
Kick:	200 your choice
Pull:	300
Benchmark Swim:	50 Backstroke
Swim:	12 x 25 – alternating Freestyle/Backstroke/Easy choice... w/15 SR
Cool down:	200
Total:	2,750

Workout 37

Tip of the Day: Use a stroke and kick rate that is equal to freestyle.

Warm up:	400
Kick:	8 x 50 Flutter Kick – alternating 50s on front/on back
Swim:	200 Freestyle
Swim:	200 – alternating 25s of Freestyle/Backstroke
Pull:	300
Swim:	10 x 50 Freestyle on your interval
Swim:	4 x 50 alternating 25s of Freestyle/Backstroke on your freestyle interval
Swim:	10 x 50 Backstroke on your interval
Cool down:	200
Total:	2,800

Workout 38

Tip of the Day: Catch deep, then throw the water towards your feet.

Warm up:	400
Kick:	8 x 50 Flutter Kick – alternating 50s on front/on back
Drill:	200 "12 Kick Switch"
Drill:	200 "One Arm Pull/Push Backstroke"
Swim:	4 x 100 Freestyle, except for last length of each 100 is Backstroke
Swim:	3 x100 Freestyle, except last 50 of each 100 is Backstroke
Swim:	2 x 100 Freestyle, except last 75 of each 100 is Backstroke

50 Easy

Benchmark Swim:	100 Backstroke

50 Easy

Benchmark Swim:	100 Freestyle

50 Easy

Kick/Swim:	12 x 25 alternating Flutter Kick on back/ Backstroke/Easy Freestyle... w/15 SR
Cool down:	200
Total:	2,950

Workout

Tip of the Day: Try reducing your 100 Backstroke interval by 5 seconds.

Warm up:	400
Kick:	6 x 25 Flutter Kick on back w/10 SR
Drill:	200 "3 Strokes/6Kicks"
Kick:	6 x 25 Flutter Kick on back w/10 SR
Swim:	3 x 100 Backstroke on your interval
Swim:	4 x 100 Freestyle on your interval
Swim:	5 x 100 Backstroke on your interval
Pull:	500
Swim:	8 x 25 Backstroke – Fast/Easy w/15 SR
Cool down:	200
Total:	3,000

Workout

Tip of the Day: Hold your pace.

Warm up:	400
Kick:	8 x 50 your choice w/10 SR
Drill:	200 "Up and Over"
Drill:	200 "Breathing Rhythm"
Swim:	20 x 50 – alternating 50s of Freestyle/Backstroke w/10 SR
Pull:	500
Benchmark Swim:	200 Backstroke
Cool down:	200
Total:	3,000

41 Workout

Tip of the Day: Think: tempo.

Warm up:	300
Kick:	8 x 50 Flutter Kick – alternating 50s on front/on back w/10 SR
Drill:	200 "Backstroke 12 Kick Switch"
Swim:	4 x 50 Backstroke – Build, on your interval
Drill:	200 "Backstroke 3 Strokes/6 Kicks"
Swim:	4 x 50 Backstroke – Build, on your interval
Swim:	4 x 100 Freestyle – Descending, on your interval
Swim:	4 x 100 Freestyle – Descending, on your interval
Benchmark Swim:	50 Backstroke
50 Easy	
Pull:	500
Benchmark Swim:	50 Freestyle
50 Easy	
Cool down:	200
Total:	3,200

Workout

Tip of the Day: Try reducing your 50 Backstroke interval by 5 seconds.

Warm up:	400
Kick:	200 Flutter Kick on front
Kick:	200 Flutter Kick on back
Swim:	10 x 50 Freestyle on your interval
Swim:	10 x 50 alternating 25s of Freestyle/Backstroke on your Freestyle interval
Swim:	10 x 50 Backstroke on your interval
Pull:	500
Kick:	8 x 25 Flutter Kick on back – alternating 25s of Fast/Easy w/15 SR
Cool down:	200
Total:	3,200

Workout

Tip of the Day: Check target heart rate.

Warm up:	400
Kick/Swim:	12 x 50 alternating 50s of Freestyle/Flutter Kick on back w/10 SR
Drill/Swim:	300 "3 Strokes/6 Kicks Backstroke"
Swim:	8 x 50 Freestyle – Build, on your interval
Swim:	8 x 50 Backstroke – Build, on your interval
Pull:	500
Benchmark Swim:	100 Backstroke
50 Easy	
Swim:	12 x 25 alternating Freestyle/Backstroke w/15 SR
Cool down:	200
Total:	3,250

44 Workout

Tip of the Day: Try inhaling on one backstroke recovery, and exhaling on the other.

Warm up:	400
Kick:	8 x 25 Flutter Kick w/10 SR
Drill:	200 "Backstroke 12 Kick Switch"
Kick:	8 x 25 Flutter Kick on back w/10 SR
Drill:	200 "Roll, Pull/Roll, Push"
Swim:	5 x 100 Freestyle – Descending, on your interval
Swim:	5 x 100 Backstroke – Descending, on your interval
Kick:	300 your choice
Swim:	4 x 50 Backstroke on your interval
Swim:	4 x 25 Fast Freestyle w/15 SR
Swim:	4 x 50 Freestyle on your interval
Swim:	4 x 25 Fast Backstroke w/15 SR
Cool down:	200
Total:	3,300

Workout 45

Tip of the Day: Make sure you are kicking up with quick power.

Warm up:	400
Kick:	200 Flutter Kick
Drill:	200 "Pigeon Toed Kicking"
Swim:	4 x 200 – alternating 25s of Freestyle/Backstroke w/20 SR
Swim:	4 x 50 Backstroke – Build, on your interval
Swim:	4 x 50 Freestyle – Descending, on your interval
Kick:	200 your choice
Benchmark Swim:	200 Backstroke
Pull:	500
Swim:	8 x 25 Backstroke – alternating Fast/Easy w/15 SR
Cool down:	200
Total:	3,300

Workout

Tip of the Day: Maintain a constant stroke count.

Warm up:	400
Kick:	200 Flutter Kick
Drill:	200 "One Arm Pull/Push Backstroke"
Swim:	200 alternating 25s of Freestyle/Backstroke
Kick:	200 Flutter Kick on back
Drill:	200 "Up and Over"
Swim:	200 Backstroke
Swim:	8 x 50 Backstroke – Build, on your interval
Swim:	8 x 50 Freestyle – Build on your interval
Pull:	5 x 100 w/15 SR
Benchmark Swim:	50 Backstroke
50 Easy	
Swim:	8 x 25 Fast Freestyle w/15 SR
Cool down:	200
Total:	3,400

47 Workout

Tip of the Day: Maintain a well-coordinated stroke.

Warm up:	400
Kick:	300 – Flutter Kick alternating 25s on front/on back
Drill:	200 "Armpit Lift"
Drill/Swim:	200 alternating 25s of "Armpit Lift"/Backstroke
Swim:	200 Backstroke
Swim:	20 x 50 Freestyle on your interval
Swim:	10 x 50 Backstroke on your interval
Kick:	200 your choice
Swim:	8 x 25 alternating 25s of Freestyle/Backstroke w/15 SR
Cool down:	200
Total:	3,400

Workout

Tip of the Day: Swim on your axis.

Warm up:	400
Kick:	100 Flutter Kick on back
Kick:	100 Flutter Kick
Kick:	100 Flutter Kick on back
Swim:	5 x 100 Freestyle – Pace, on your interval
Pull:	500
Swim:	5 x 100 – alternating 50s of Backstroke/Freestyle

50 Easy
Benchmark Swim: 100 Backstroke
50 Easy

Swim:	8 x 50 Free Descending on your interval
Swim:	6 x 50 alternating 25s of Freestyle/Backstroke on your freestyle interval
Swim:	4 x 50 Fast Backstroke on your interval
Cool down:	200
Total:	3,500

Workout

Tip of the Day: Maintain constant stroke and kicking motion.

Warm up:	400
Kick:	200 – your choice
Drill:	4 x 50 "Backstroke 12 Kick Switch" w/15 SR
Swim:	12 x 100 Freestyle – Descending interval every fourth 100
Pull:	500
Swim:	5 x 100 Backstroke on your interval
Kick/Swim:	6 x 50 Flutter Kick – alternating on front/on back w/10 SR
Cool down:	200
Total:	3,500

50Workout

Tip of the Day: Maintain length of stroke.

Warm up:	400
Kick:	200 Flutter Kick
Drill:	200 your choice
Kick:	200 Flutter Kick on back
Swim:	8 x 50 Freestyle – Build, on your interval
Swim:	8 x 50 – alternating 25s of Freestyle/Backstroke w/10 SR
Swim:	8 x 50 Backstroke on your interval
Benchmark Swim:	200 Backstroke
Pull:	500
Kick:	200 your choice
Benchmark Swim:	200 Freestyle
Cool down:	200
Total:	3,500

WORKOUTS
BREASTSTROKE

Shape Up Workouts for Breaststroke

Workout

Tip of the Day: Minimize drag by maximizing streamline.

Warm up:	400
Kick:	200 other than breaststroke kick
Drill:	200 "3 Kick Breaststroke"
Drill:	200 "Breaststroke with Dolphin"
Drill/Swim:	200 alternating 25s of "Breaststroke with Dolphin"/Breaststroke
Swim:	10 x 50 alternating 25s of Freestyle/Breaststroke w/10 SR
Benchmark Swim:	50 Breaststroke
Kick:	4 x 25 Breaststroke Kick w/10 SR
Swim:	4 x 25 Breaststroke w/15 SR
Cool down:	200
Total:	2,250

Workout

Tip of the Day: Establish a 50 Breaststroke interval.

Warm up:	400
Kick:	200 other than breaststroke kick
Drill:	200 "Breaststroke Alternating Dolphin and Breaststroke Kick"
Swim:	10 x 50 Freestyle on your interval
Swim:	10 x 50 Breaststroke on your interval
Kick:	4 x 25 Breaststroke Kick
Swim:	200 Breaststroke
Cool down:	200
Total:	2,300

Workout

Tip of the Day: Work the kick!

Warm up:	400
Kick:	200 other than breaststroke kick
Kick:	200 Breaststroke Kick
Drill:	200 "3 Kick Breaststroke"
Drill:	200 "Stroke Up To Breathe, Kick Down to Glide"
Swim:	6 x 100 alternating 100s of Freestyle/Breaststroke w/15 SR
Swim:	8 x 25 Breaststroke – Fast/Easy w/15 SR
Benchmark Swim:	100 Breaststroke
Cool down:	200
Total:	2,300

54 Workout

Tip of the Day: Establish a 100 Breaststroke interval.

Warm up:	400
Kick:	200 other than breaststroke kick
Drill:	200 "Breaststroke with Dolphin"
Drill:	200 "Breaststroke Alternating Dolphin and Breaststroke Kick"
Drill/Swim:	4 x 25 alternating Choice Drill/Breaststroke
Swim:	200 alternating 100s of Freestyle/Breaststroke
Swim:	5 x 100 Breaststroke on your interval
Kick/Swim:	8 x 25 alternating Breaststroke Kick/Breaststroke w/15 SR
Cool down:	200
Total:	2,400

55 Workout

Tip of the Day: Maintain a consistent stroke count.

Warm up:	400
Kick:	8 x 50 other than breaststroke kick w/10 SR
Drill:	200 "Corner Drill"
Drill:	200 "Breaststroke with Dolphin"
Swim:	4 x 50 Freestyle on your interval
Swim:	4 x 50 Breaststroke on your interval
Swim:	4 x 50 Freestyle on your interval
Swim:	4 x 50 Breaststroke on your interval
Benchmark Swim:	200 Breaststroke
Cool down:	200
Total:	2,400

Workout

Tip of the Day: Shoot to streamline.

Warm up:	400
Kick:	200 other than breaststroke kick
Drill:	200 "Breaststroke with Dolphin"
Drill:	200 "Stroke Up to Breathe, Kick Down to Glide"
Drill:	200 "Shoot to Streamline"
Swim:	5 x 100 Freestyle on your interval
Pull:	500 Freestyle
Benchmark Swim:	50 Breaststroke
Kick:	4 x 25 Breaststroke Kick
Cool down:	200
Total:	2,550

57 Workout

Tip of the Day: Find leverage from head to hips.

Warm up:	400
Kick:	300 other than breaststroke kick w/10 SR
Drill:	4 x 50 "Breaststroke with Dolphin" w/10 SR
Drill/Swim:	200 alternating 25s of "Breaststroke with Dolphin"/ Breaststroke
Drill:	4 x 25 "Eyes on the Water" w/10 SR
Swim:	10 x 50 Freestyle – descending even 50s, on your Interval
Swim:	10 x 50 Breaststroke – descending even 50s, on your interval
Kick:	6 x 25 Breaststroke Kick w/10 SR
Cool down:	200
Total:	2,550

58 Workout

Tip of the Day: Keep arm stroke small and forward.

Warm up:	400
Kick:	200 other than breaststroke kick
Swim:	10 x 50 Freestyle – Build, on your interval
Drill:	4 x 50 "Hand Speed Drill" w/15 SR
Swim:	200 Breaststroke
Drill:	4 x 50 "Corners Drill" w/15 SR
Swim:	200 Breaststroke
Pull:	400
Benchmark Swim:	100 Breaststroke
Cool down:	200
Total:	2,600

59 Workout

Tip of the Day: Find your rhythm and hold on to it.

Warm up:	400
Kick:	300 other than breaststroke kick
Swim:	5 x 100 Freestyle on your interval
Swim:	500 Breaststroke
Kick:	200 your choice
Swim:	5 x 100 Breaststroke on your interval
Cool down:	200
Total:	2,600

Workout

Tip of the Day: Exhale during the power phase of the kick.

Warm up:	400
Kick:	200 other than breaststroke kick
Drill:	200 "Breaststroke with Dolphin"
Drill:	200 "Shoot to Streamline"
Swim:	2 x 100 Freestyle – Descending, on your interval
Swim:	3 x 100 Breaststroke – Descending, on your interval
Swim:	4 x 100 Freestyle – Descending, on your interval
Swim:	5 x 100 Breaststroke – Descending, on your interval
Cool down:	200
Total:	2,600

Workout

Tip of the Day: Hold on to the water during outsweep and insweep.

Warm up:	400
Kick:	300 other than breaststroke kick
Drill:	8 x 25 "Hand Speed" w/10 SR
Drill:	4 x 50 "Corners Drill" w/15 SR
Swim:	200 Breaststroke

Swim: 5 x 100 Freestyle and Breaststroke w/15 SR
1) All Freestyle
2) 75 Freestyle + 25 Breaststroke
3) 50 Freestyle + 50 Breaststroke
4) 25 Freestyle + 75 Breaststroke
5) All Breaststroke

Pull 500
50 Easy
Benchmark Swim: 50 Breaststroke
50 Easy
Benchmark Swim: 50 Freestyle

Cool down: 200

Total: 2,700

Workout

Tip of the Day: Try to reduce your 50 Breaststroke interval.

Warm up:	400
Kick:	300 other than breaststroke kick
Swim:	300 Freestyle – every third length fast
Kick:	200 Breaststroke Kick
Swim:	300 Freestyle – every other length fast
Kick:	200 Breaststroke Kick
Swim:	300 Freestyle – all fast
50 Easy	
Swim:	10 x 50 Breaststroke – Build, on your interval
Cool down:	200
Total:	2,700

Workout

Tip of the Day: Raise your chest to breathe, not your chin.

Warm up:	400
Kick:	8 x 25 other than breaststroke kick w/10 SR
Drill:	8 x 50 "Eyes on the Water" w/10 SR
Swim:	4 x 200 alternating 200s of Freestyle/Breaststroke w/15 SR
50 Easy	
Benchmark Swim:	100 Breaststroke
50 Easy	
Benchmark Swim:	100 Freestyle
Kick:	200 Choice
Swim:	12 x 25 alternating Freestyle/Breaststroke
Cool down:	200
Total:	2,800

64 Workout

Tip of the Day: Strike streamline between each new stroke.

Warm up:	400
Kick:	200 – other than breaststroke kick
Swim:	5 x 100 Freestyle – Descending, on your interval
Drill:	4 x 50 "Thread the Needle" w/10 SR
Drill:	4 x 50 "Hand Speed Drill" w/10 SR
Pull:	300
Swim:	5 x 100 Breaststroke – Descending, on your interval
50 Easy	
Swim:	4 x 50 Freestyle – Descending, on your interval
Swim:	4 x 50 Breaststroke – Descending, on your interval
Cool down:	200
Total:	2,950

65 Workout

Tip of the Day: Breathe at the natural high point of the stroke.

Warm up:	400
Kick:	200 other than breaststroke kick
Drill:	200 "Breaststroke with Dolphin"
Drill:	200 "Corners Drill"
Drill:	200 "Stroke Up to Breathe, Kick Down to Glide"
Swim:	6 x 50 Freestyle – Build, on your interval
Swim:	4 x 50 Breaststroke – Build, on your interval
Swim:	8 x 50 Freestyle – Descending even 50s, on your interval
Swim:	6 x 50 Breaststroke – Descending even 50s, on your interval

50 Easy

Benchmark Swim:	200 Breaststroke
Cool down:	200
Total:	2,950

# Workout

Tip of the Day: Thread the needle.

Warm up:	400
Kick:	300 other than breaststroke kick
Swim:	8 x 50 Freestyle – Build, on your interval
Drill:	8 x 50 "Thread the Needle" w/ 15 SR
Pull:	300
Drill:	200 "Breaststroke with Dolphin"
Benchmark Swim:	50 Breaststroke
Kick:	300 your choice
Benchmark Swim:	50 Breaststroke
50 Easy	
Swim:	14 x 25 alternating 25s of Freestyle/Breaststroke w/15 SR
Cool down:	200
Total:	3,000

Workout 67

Tip of the Day: Check your target heart rate.

Warm up:	400
Kick:	8 x 50 w/10 SR other than breaststroke kick
Swim:	10 x 50 Freestyle – Build, on your interval
Pull:	200
Swim:	200 Breaststroke
Swim:	100 Breaststroke
Swim:	50 Breaststroke
Swim:	100 Breaststroke
Swim:	200 Breaststroke
Swim:	10 x 50 Breaststroke – Build, on your interval
Pull:	200
Cool down:	200
Total:	3,050

Workout

Tip of the Day: Accelerate your kick!

Warm up:	400
Kick:	200 Flutter Kick
Drill:	200 "Breaststroke Alternating Dolphin and Breast-stroke Kick"
Drill:	200 "Stroke Up to Breathe, Kick Down to Glide"
Swim:	8 x 50 Freestyle – Build, on your interval
Pull:	500
Swim:	8 x 50 Breaststroke – Build, on your interval

50 Easy

Swim:	4 x 25 Breaststroke w/15 SR

50 Easy

Benchmark Swim:	100 Breaststroke

50 Easy

Swim:	8 x 25 Breaststroke w/10 SR – achieve power from the core
Cool down:	200
Total:	3,050

Workout

Tip of the Day: Use available leverage from your core.

Warm up:	400
Kick:	200 other than breaststroke kick
Swim:	3 x 200 Freestyle – Descending, w/20 SR
Drill:	200 "Breaststroke with Dolphin"
Drill/Swim:	6 x 50 alternating "Breaststroke with Dolphin"/ Breaststroke w/15 SR
Swim:	200 Breaststroke
	3 x 100 Freestyle – Descending, on your interval
	5 x 100 Breaststroke – Descending, on your interval
	3 x 100 Freestyle – Descending, on your interval
Cool down:	200
Total:	3,200

# Workout

Tip of the Day: Pull and breathe, then kick and glide.

Warm up:	400
Kick:	200 other than breaststroke kick
Swim:	8 x 25 Freestyle – Build w/10 SR
Swim:	8 x 25 Breaststroke – Build, with 10 SR
Pull:	500
Benchmark Swim: 50 Easy	200 Breaststroke
Kick:	200 your choice
Swim:	5 x 100 Freestyle – Descending, on your interval
Swim:	12 x 50 Breaststroke – on Descending Interval 4 x 50 – Pace on your interval 4 x 50 – Pace on your interval minus 5 seconds 4 x 50 – Pace on your interval minus 10 seconds
Cool down:	200
Total:	3,350

Workout

Tip of the Day: Think sequence and coordination.

Warm up:	400
Kick:	300 other than breaststroke kick
Swim:	4 x 75 – Freestyle – Build, w/15 SR
Drill:	200 "Stroke Up to Breathe, Kick Down to Glide"
Swim:	200 Breaststroke
Drill:	200 "Thread the Needle"
Swim:	200 Breaststroke
Drill:	200 "Shoot to Streamline"
Swim:	4 x 75 – Freestyle – Build, w/15 SR
Benchmark Swim:	50 Breaststroke
Kick:	200 your choice
Swim:	4 x 75 – Breaststroke – Build, w/15 SR
Benchmark Swim:	50 Freestyle
Swim:	4 x 75 – Breaststroke – Build, w/15 SR
Cool down:	200
Total:	3,400

 Workout

Tip of the Day: Increase your stroke tempo.

Warm up:	400
Drill/Swim:	300 "Hand Speed Drill"/Breaststroke
Swim:	4 x 50 Freestyle – Build, on your interval
Swim:	10 x 50 Breaststroke – Build, on your interval
Pull:	200
Swim:	4 x 50 Freestyle – Descend even 50s, on your interval
Swim:	10 x 50 Breaststroke – Descend even 50s, on your interval
Pull:	200
Swim:	8 x 50 Freestyle – on Descending Interval 4 x 50 – Pace, on your interval 4 x 50 – Pace, on your interval minus 5 seconds
Swim:	8 x 50 Breaststroke – on Descending Interval 4 x 50 – Pace, on your interval 4 x 50 – Pace, on your interval minus 5 seconds
Cool down:	200
Total:	3,500

Workout

Tip of the Day: Build to a sustainable pace.

Warm up:	400
Kick:	300 other than breaststroke kick
Drill:	4 x 50 "Hand Speed Drill" w/10 SR
Drill:	200 "Breaststroke with Dolphin"
Swim:	6 x 100 Freestyle on Descending Interval (30 SR descending 5 seconds each repeat)
Swim:	Breaststroke Pyramid – 25, 50, 75, 100, 150, 200, 150, 100, 75, 50, 25 w/15 SR
Kick:	200 your choice
Pull:	300
Benchmark Swim:	100 Breaststroke
Cool down:	200
Total:	3,500

74 Workout

Tip of the Day: Accelerate through the arm stroke, accelerate through the kick.

Warm up:	400
Kick:	200 other than breaststroke kick
Swim:	4 x 50 Freestyle – Build, on your interval
Drill:	100 "Corners Drill"
Drill:	100 "3 Kick Breaststroke"
Swim:	3 x 300 w/30 SR
	1) 50 Freestyle + 25 Breaststroke...
	2) 25 Freestyle + 50 Breaststroke...
	3) all Breaststroke
Pull:	500
Swim:	5 x 100 Breaststroke – Pace, on your interval
Kick:	200 your choice
Swim:	8 x 25 Breaststroke w/15 SR
Cool down:	200
Total:	3,500

75 Workout

Tip of the Day: Achieve stealth Breaststroke.

Warm up:	200
Kick:	200 – other than breaststroke kick
Swim:	8 x 50 – Build, on your interval
Drill:	200 "Shoot to Streamline"
Drill:	200 "Thread the Needle"
Drill:	200 "Eyes on the Water"
Swim:	500 alternating 25s of Freestyle/Breaststroke
Pull:	5 x 100 w/15 SR
Drill:	200 "Breaststroke with Dolphin"
Benchmark Swim:	200 Breaststroke
50 Easy	
Kick:	200 your choice
50 Easy	
Benchmark Swim:	200 Freestyle
Cool down:	200
Total:	3,500

WORKOUTS
BUTTERFLY

Shape Up Workouts for Butterfly

76 Workout

Tip of the Day: Achieve a fluid full body dolphin motion.

Warm up:	400
Kick:	400 Flutter Kick
Kick:	4 x 50 Dolphin – head leading w/10 SR
Kick:	4 x 50 Dolphin – hands leading w/10 SR
Swim:	4 x 100 Freestyle – Pace, on your interval
Drill/Swim:	8 x 50 – alternating 25s of "One Arm Butterfly"/ Freestyle w/15 SR

50 Easy

Benchmark Swim:	25 Butterfly
Cool down:	200
Total:	2,225

77 Workout

Tip of the Day: Strive for a chest down, hips up position to start each stroke.

Warm up:	400
Kick:	200 Flutter Kick
Kick:	200 Dolphin – head leading
Swim:	5 x 100 Freestyle – Pace, on your interval
Drill:	200 "One Arm Butterfly"
Drill:	200 "Advanced One Arm Butterfly"
50 Easy	
Swim:	4 x 25 Butterfly w/30 SR
50 Easy	
Swim:	4 x 25 Freestyle w/15 SR
Cool down:	200
Total:	2,200

Workout

Tip of the Day: Stroke from front to back, avoid pressing down!

Warm up:	400
Kick:	300 Flutter Kick
Drill:	8 x 25 "One Arm Butterfly" w/15 SR
Kick:	200 Dolphin alternating 25s of head leading/ hands leading
Drill:	8 x 25 "Advanced One Arm Butterfly"w/15 SR
Swim:	4 x 100 Freestyle – Descending, on your interval
Pull:	300
50 Easy	
Benchmark Swim:	50 Butterfly
Cool down:	200
Total:	2,300

Workout

Tip of the Day: Maintain a rhythmic dolphin action.

Warm up:	400
Kick:	200 Flutter Kick
Kick:	200 Dolphin – head leading
Kick:	200 Flutter Kick
Kick:	200 Dolphin – hands leading
Swim:	10 x 50 Freestyle – Build, on your interval
50 Easy	
Swim:	8 x 50 alternating 25s of Butterfly/Choice w/20 SR
Cool down:	200
Total:	2,350

Workout

Tip of the Day: Use your abdominals.

Warm up:	400
Kick:	400 alternating Flutter Kick/Dolphin – head leading
Drill:	4 x 50 "One Arm Butterfly" w/15 SR
Swim:	4 x 50 alternating 25s of Butterfly/Freestyle
Drill:	4 x 50 "Advanced One Arm Butterfly" w/15 SR
Pull:	500
Swim:	3 x 100 alternating 25s of Butterfly/Breaststroke w/30 SR
Cool down:	200
Total:	2,400

Workout 81

Tip of the Day: Dolphins don't have knees.

Warm up:	400
Kick:	300 Dolphin – head leading
Kick:	300 Flutter Kick
Drill/Swim:	8 x 25 alternating 25s of "One Arm Butterfly"/ Freestyle w/20 SR
Drill/Swim:	8 x 25 alternating 25s of "Advanced One Arm Butterfly"/Freestyle w/20 SR
Drill:	8 x 25 alternating 25s of "One Arm Butterfly"/ "Advanced One Arm Butterfly w/20 SR
Drill/Swim:	8 x 25 alternating 25s of choice drill/Butterfly w/20 SR
Swim:	6 x 50 Freestyle – Pace, on your interval
Pull:	200
Benchmark Swim:	25 Butterfly
Cool down:	200
Total:	2,525

Workout

Tip of the Day: Reach for a "Y".

Warm up:	400
Kick:	10 x 50 – alternating Flutter Kick/Dolphin – head leading w/10 SR
Drill:	8 x 25 alternating 25s of "Reaching to a "Y"/One Arm Butterfly" w/15 SR
Swim:	5 x 100 Freestyle – Descending, on your interval
Pull:	5 x 100 w/15 SR
Swim:	4 x 25 Butterfly w/30 SR
50 Easy	
Swim:	4 x 25 Butterfly w/30 SR
Cool down:	200
Total:	2,550

Workout

Tip of the Day: Breathe low, and look at the water while breathing.

Warm up:	400
Kick:	6 x 50 Flutter Kick w/10 SR
Swim:	4 x 100 Freestyle – Build, on your interval
Drill:	4 x 25 "Reaching to a "Y" – w/20 SR
50 Easy	
Drill:	4 x 25 "Hammer and Nail" – w/20 SR
50 Easy	
Drill:	4 x 25 "Chest Balance" – w/20 SR – trace deep to shallow question marks
50 Easy	
Drill:	4 x 50 alternating 25s of "One Arm Butterfly"/ "Advanced One Arm Butterfly" w/20 SR
Swim:	4 x 100 Freestyle – Descending, on your interval
Pull:	200
50 Easy	
Benchmark Swim:	50 Butterfly
Cool down:	200
Total:	2,650

84 Workout

Tip of the Day: Kick to start the stroke, kick to finish the stroke.

Warm up:	400
Kick:	400 alternating 50s of Flutter Kick/Dolphin – hand leading
Drill:	200 "One Arm Fly"
Drill:	200 "Advanced One Arm Fly"
Drill:	4 x 25 "Coordination Checkpoint" w/30 SR
Swim:	5 x 100 – 25 Butterfly + 75 Freestyle w/30 SR
Kick:	300 your choice
Swim:	2 x 50 Butterfly w/20 SR
Swim:	2 x 50 Freestyle w/15 SR
Swim:	2 x 50 Butterfly w/20 SR
Swim:	2 x 50 Freestyle w/15 SR
Cool down:	200
Total:	2,700

Workout

Tip of the Day: Maintain a relaxed recovery with pinkies up!

Warm up:	400
Kick:	200 alternating 25s of Dolphin – head leading/ Flutter Kick
Swim:	8 x 50 Freestyle – Build, on your interval
Drill:	4 x 50 "One Arm Butterfly" w/15 SR
Swim:	8 x 50 Freestyle – Descend even 50s, on your interval
Drill:	4 x 50 "Advanced One Arm Butterfly" w/15 SR
Swim:	8 x 50 Freestyle – Pace, on your interval
Drill:	4 x 50 "Left Arm, Right Arm, Both Arms" with 15 SR
Benchmark Swim:	100 Butterfly
Cool down:	200
Total:	2,700

Workout

Tip of the Day: Reach, but don't stop the stroke in front... Grab and go!

Warm up:	400
Kick:	400 your choice
Drill/Swim:	4 x 50 ""One Arm Butterfly"/Freestyle w/15 SR
Drill/Swim:	4 x 50 "Reaching to a "Y"/Freestyle w/15 SR
Drill/Swim:	4 x 50 "Coordination Checkpoint"/Freestyle w/15 SR
Swim/Pull:	4 x 200 alternating 200s of Freestyle/Pull w/20 SR
Kick:	200 Dolphin alternating 25s of head leading/ hands leading

50 Easy

Benchmark Swim:	25 Butterfly

50 Easy

Benchmark Swim:	25 Butterfly
Cool down:	200
Total:	2,750

87 Workout

Tip of the Day: Swim like you have no bones.

Warm up:	400
Kick:	200 Flutter Kick
Kick:	8 x 25 dolphin alternating 25s of head leading/ hands leading w/10 SR
Swim:	6 x 50 Freestyle – build, on your interval
Drill:	4 x 25 "The Flop" w/20 SR
Swim:	6 x 50 Freestyle – descending, on your interval
Drill:	4 x 25 "Chest Balance" w/20 SR
Swim:	6 x 50 Freestyle – pace, on your interval
Kick:	200 your choice
Pull:	200
Swim:	4 x 25 Butterfly – establish an interval
50 Easy	
Swim:	4 x 25 Butterfly on your interval
Cool down:	200
Total:	2,850

Workout

Tip of the Day: Achieve a relaxed recovery.

Warm up:	400
Kick:	8 x 50 alternating 50s of Flutter Kick/Dolphin w/10 SR
Drill/Swim:	8 x 25 "The Flop"/Freestyle w/15 SR
Drill/Swim:	8 x 25 "Pinkies Up"/Freestyle w/15 SR
Swim:	4 x 100 Freestyle, except first length of each 100 is Butterfly w/ 15 SR
50 Easy	
Swim:	4 x 100 Freestyle, except last length of each 100 is Butterfly w/ 15 SR
Kick:	200 your choice
Pull:	200
Benchmark Swim:	50 Butterfly
50 Easy	
Swim:	8 x 25 alternating 25s of Butterfly/Choice w/15 SR
Cool down:	200
Total:	2,900

Workout

Tip of the Day: Swim forward, not up and down.

Warm up:	400
Kick:	200 your choice
Swim:	4 x 25 "One Arm Butterfly" w/15 SR
Swim:	4 x 100 Freestyle – Pace, on your interval
Drill:	4 x 25 "One Arm Butterfly" w/15 SR
Swim:	4 x 100 Freestyle – Pace, on your interval
Drill:	4 x 25 "Advanced One Arm Butterfly" w/15 SR
Swim:	4 x 100 Freestyle – Pace, on your interval
Kick:	200 your choice
Swim:	8 x 50 Butterfly – establish an interval
Cool down:	200
Total:	2,900

Workout

Tip of the Day: Start breathing early. Get head back down before hands finish recovery.

Warm up:	400
Kick:	200 Flutter Kick
Kick:	200 Dolphin – alternating 25s of head leading/ hands leading
Swim:	5 x 100 Freestyle – Descending, on your interval
Drill:	300 alternating 25s of "One Arm Butterfly"/ "Advanced One Arm butterfly"
Pull:	300
Swim:	25 Fly, 50 Free, 75 Fly, 100 Free, 75 Fly, 50 Free, 25 Fly w/20 SR
Kick:	8 x 50 your choice w/10 SR
Benchmark Swim:	100 Butterfly
Cool down:	200
Total:	3,000

# Workout

Tip of the Day: Try to see yourself advancing through the water as you breathe.

Warm up:	400
Kick:	400 Flutter Kick – alternating 25s of Fast/Easy
Swim:	12 x 100 Freestyle – on Descending Interval – after every three 100s
Drill/Swim:	8 x 25 alternating 25s of "Hammer and Nail"/ Freestyle w/15 SR
Drill/Swim:	8 x 25 alternating 25s of "Reaching to a "Y"/ Freestyle w/15 SR
Drill/Swim:	8 x 25 alternating 25s of "The Flop"/Freestyle w/15 SR

50 Easy

Benchmark Swim:	25 Butterfly
Kick:	6 x 25 Flutter Kick w/15 SR
Cool down:	200
Total:	3,025

Workout

Tip of the Day: Inhale at the natural high point of the stroke.

Warm up:	400
Drill/Swim:	200 alternating 25s of "One Arm Butterfly"/ Free-style
Kick:	200 your choice
Drill/Swim:	200 alternating 25s of "Coordination Checkpoint"/ Freestyle
Kick:	200 your choice
Swim:	5 x 100 Freestyle – Descending, on your interval
Pull:	300
Swim:	5 x 100 Freestyle – Descending, on your interval
Pull:	300
Swim:	8 x 25 Butterfly – on your interval
Cool down:	200
Total:	3,200

Workout

Tip of the Day: Catch wide and high. Your chest should be lower than your hands when you catch.

Warm up:	400
Kick:	6 x 50 your choice w/10 SR
Swim:	6 x 50 Freestyle – Build, on your interval
Drill/Swim:	200 alternating 25s of "Advanced One Arm Butterfly"/Freestyle
Drill/Swim:	200 alternating 25s of "Reaching to a "Y"/Freestyle
Drill/Swim:	200 alternating 25s of "The Flop"/Freestyle
Swim:	3 x 100 Freestyle – Descending, on your interval
Kick:	200 your choice
Swim:	3 x 100 Freestyle – Descending, on your interval
Pull:	300
Swim:	3 x 100 Freestyle – Descending, on your interval
Benchmark Swim:	50 Butterfly
Cool down:	200
Total:	3,250

Workout

Tip of the Day: Shift your weight forward to catch.

Warm up:	400
Kick:	300 your choice
Swim:	4 x 100 Freestyle – Build, on your interval
Swim:	4 x 100 Freestyle – Descending, on your interval
Drill:	200 "Advanced One Arm Butterfly"
Drill/Swim:	8 x 50 alternating 25s of "Chest Balance"/Freestyle w/15 SR
Drill/Swim:	8 x 50 alternating 25s of "Reaching to a "Y"/Freestyle w/15 SR
Kick:	200 Dolphin – head leading
Swim:	8 x 50 Butterfly on your interval
Cool down:	200
Total:	3,300

95 Workout

Tip of the Day: After breathing, get your back into the line of the stroke.

Warm up:	400
Kick:	10 x 50 alternating 50s of Flutter/Dolphin – head leading
Swim/Pull:	4 x 200 alternating 200s of Freestyle/Pull w/20 SR
Drill/Swim:	8 x 25 alternating 25 of "The Flop"/Freestyle w/15 SR
Drill/Swim:	8 x 25 alternating 25 of "Hammer and Nail"/Freestyle w/15 SR
Swim:	10 x 50 Freestyle – Pace, on your interval
Kick:	200 your choice
Benchmark Swim:	100 Butterfly
Cool down:	200
Total:	3,300

Workout

Tip of the Day: Try different breathing patterns.

Warm up:	400
Kick:	300 your choice
Swim:	400 Freestyle – every third length Fast

Swim: 5 x 100 Freestyle on your interval
1) Breathe every 2 strokes
2) Breathe every 3 strokes
3) Breathe every 4 strokes
4) Breathe every 5 strokes
5) Breathe your choice

50 Easy

Swim: 4 x 50 Butterfly on your interval
1) Breathe every stroke
2) Breathe every 2 strokes
3) Breathe every 3 strokes
4) Breathe your choice

50 Easy

Kick:	8 x 50 your choice w/10 SR
Pull:	500

50 Easy

Benchmark Swim: 25 Butterfly

50 Easy

Kick: 8 x 25 fast Dolphin – hands leading w/15 SR

Cool down: 200

Total: 3,325

Workout

Tip of the Day: Make a clean entry, and balance on your chest.

Warm up:	400
Kick:	10 x 50 your choice w/10 SR
Swim:	6 x 50 Freestyle – Build, on your interval
Pull:	300
Swim:	6 x 50 Freestyle – Pace, on your interval
Pull:	300
Swim:	6 x 50 Freestyle – Descending, on your interval
Drill:	200 "One Arm Butterfly"
Drill:	200 "Advanced One Arm Butterfly"
Drill:	4 x 25 "Left Arm, Right Arm, Both Arms" w/15 SR
Drill:	4 x 25 "Chest Balance" w/15 SR
50 Easy	
Swim:	8 x 25 Butterfly on your interval
Cool down:	200
Total:	3,450

Workout

Tip of the Day: Coordination: kick and catch, kick and push.

Warm up:	400
Kick:	400 Flutter Kick – every third length fast
Drill:	8 x 50 "Freestyle One Arm Pull/Push" w/15 SR
Drill:	8 x 50 "One Arm Butterfly" w/15 SR
Swim:	4 x 200 Freestyle, except one 50 is Butterfly

  1) Last 50 on first 200
  2) Third 50 on second 200
  3) Second 50 on third 200
  4) First 50 on fourth 200

50 Easy	
Pull:	300
Kick:	10 x 50 your choice w/10 SR
Benchmark Swim:	50 Butterfly
Cool down:	200
Total:	3,500

 # Workout

Tip of the Day: Set the rhythm of the stroke and hold on to it.

Warm up:	400
Kick:	200 Flutter Kick
Drill:	200 alternating 25s of "One Arm Butterfly"/ "Advanced One Arm Butterfly"
Kick:	200 Flutter Kick
Drill:	200 alternating 25s of "Freestyle with Dolphin"/ "Left Arm, Right Arm, Both Arms"
Kick:	200 Flutter Kick
Swim/Pull:	Pyramid – 50 Freestyle, 100 Pull, 150 Freestyle, 200 Pull, 150 Freestyle, 100 Pull, 50 Freestyle w/15 SR
50 Easy	
Kick:	200 your choice
Swim:	8 x 50 Butterfly on your interval
50 Easy	
Swim:	8 x 50 Choice on your interval
Cool down:	200
Total:	3,500

Workout

Tip of the Day: Achieve quiet Butterfly – Lay your hands out on the surface instead of slapping them downward.

Warm up:	400
Kick:	8 x 50 Flutter Kick w/10 SR
Kick/Swim:	12 x 50 alternating 25s of Flutter Kick/Freestyle w/10 SR
Swim:	16 x 50 Freestyle – on Descending interval, after every fourth 50

50 Easy

Drill/Swim:	4 x 50 alternating 25s of "Advanced One Arm Butterfly"/Freestyle w/15 SR
Drill/Swim:	4 x 50 alternating 25s of "Reaching to a "Y"/ Freestyle w/15 SR
Drill/Swim:	4 x 50 alternating 25s of "Chest Balance"/ Freestyle w/15 SR
Drill/Swim:	4 x 50 alternating 25s of "The Flop"/Freestyle w/15 SR
Benchmark Swim:	100 Butterfly

50 Easy

Benchmark Swim:	100 Freestyle
Cool down:	200
Total:	3,500

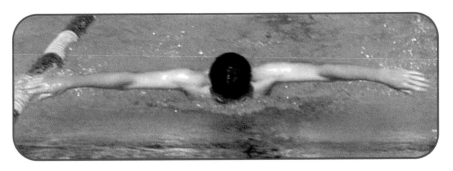

CONCLUSION

If you have completed every workout in this book, you have swum over 289,000 yards, or just over 162 miles in your quest to shape up. Congratulations!

Take a look back over your journey, and remember how you felt at the beginning. Look at yourself now! Look at your progress as shown in your Swimmer's Record. GOOD WORK!

With the fitness you have built, you may be asking yourself, "What's next?" The answer is: The sky is the limit!

CREDITS

Cover design: Sabine Groten
Cover pictures: © Christophe Schmid/fotolia.com (swimmers)
                   © Irina Belousa/fotolia.com
Illustrations: Blythe Lucero
Photography: Blythe Lucero, Vince Corbella, Gary Oto

Swimmers appearing in the photos (in alphabetical order): Mimi Abers, Meredith Anderson, Vicky Augustine, Nava Bearson, Pam Bennett, Scott Berkowitz, Conny Bleul-Gohlke, Kathryn Cohen, Monique Comacchio, Saio Costantino, Gin Daniels, Silvie Dumas, Sophia Emmonds-Bell, Lessly Field, Kathryn Fletcher, Seth Goddard, Caroline Howard, Laura Howard, Lydia Howard, Simone Howard, Tami Kasamatsu, Eric Johnson, Blythe Lucero, Bonnie Lucero, Elise Lusk, Mary Moorhead, Kim O'Keefe, Kaya Owans, Alvaro Pastor, Ida Price, Juliana Price, Zach Price, Eric Rhodes, Dave Robert, Morgan Rose, Dove Shearer, James Shum, Miranda Sinsheimer, Gabe Sturges, Steve Sturges, Sarah Tuma, Spencer Tuma

Competence in Swimming

Blythe Lucero
The 100 Best Swimming Drills

Swimming drills allow a swimmer to concentrate on a single aspect of a stroke at one time. The book is organized into sections covering the four competitive strokes: freestyle, backstroke, breaststroke and butterfly. Each drill is explained step-by-step and accompanied by comprehensive diagrams. Drill feedback charts are included to help swimmers identify problems and make modifications. Underwater and surface photographs give swimmers optimal images to emulate as they practice.

2nd edition
280 pages, full-color print
124 color photos,
137 illustrations, 100 charts
Paperback, 6^1/2" x 9^1/4"
ISBN: 978-1-84126-216-1
$ 19.95 US / $ 32.95 AUS
£ 12.95 UK/€ 19.95

photos: Frank Trautvetter © Fotolia.com

Blythe Lucero
Technique Swim Workouts

100 workouts focus on improving general swimming efficiency, with specific workouts for each of the competitive swimming strokes. The workouts in this book blend swimming drills and conditioning sets that total up to 2,000 yards/meters. Each workout is accompanied by a "Focus Point" to help swimmers zero in on stroke improvements by eliminating drag, improving feel for the water, and swimming in a core-centered manner.

160 pages, full-color print
106 photos
30 illustrations
Paperback, 6^1/2" x 9^1/4"
ISBN: 978-1-84126-268-0
$ 16.95 US / $ 29.95 AUS
£ 12.95 UK/€ 16.95

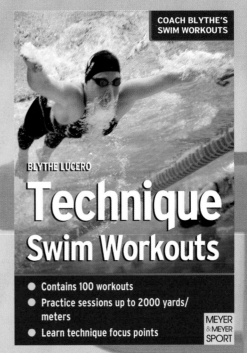

The Sports Publisher

MEYER
& MEYER
SPORT

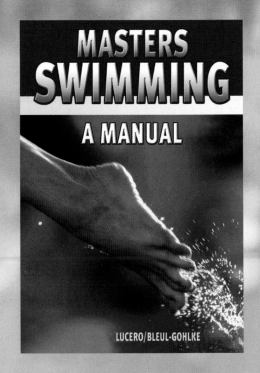